*Wake Up Dummy....
It's Me, GOD!*

Linda Habisreitinger

Cover photo of nature trails in Jean Lafitte National Historical Park and Preserve, courtesy of Sandra and Robert Pace, Pace PicturesHD
Copyright © 2014 Linda Habisreitinger

All rights reserved.

ISBN: 10: 1497356628
ISBN-13: 978-1497356627

DEDICATION

For Gary, Rhonda, Bonnie and Sandra, Robbie, Shirley, Omer and Randy. I pray that we will all be together in Paradise.

Amen.

CONTENTS

Acknowledgments

Forward

1	Wake Up Number One	1
2	Love At First Sight	19
3	Gary and Me	25
4	Military Life	49
5	Germany and The Witnesses	79
6	The Atheist	123
7	Betrayal and Forgiveness	143
8	The Business Woman	151
9	Death and Regrets	173
10	Rise of The Tea Party	185
11	Wake Up and Live	219
12	The Plan	247
	Conclusion	275

ACKNOWLEDGMENTS

Without the help of my family and friends, I would never have been able to finish this project. Most of all, I must acknowledge Jehovah-Jireh "The Lord Our Provider" without whom I would not have had anything to write.

FORWARD

When God speaks, you had better listen or you are a dummy. Well, I will tell you, I'm no dummy. I don't mean to actually say God has called me one, even though I have done some dumb things in my life. I just wanted to have a happy, normal life. My life wasn't normal for many years. At some point, I thought I had gotten my wish and all seemed right and *normal*. As sometimes happens, life threw us a curve. On December 17th, 2010 my loving husband had to make a decision that would change our lives forever. I don't know if that had anything to do with God's plan for me and our family but it wouldn't surprise me because of the changes it brought about for all of us.

So many of the things that happen in our lives follow a trail that begins when we aren't paying attention. We may scratch our head and ask, "*How in the world did this happen to me?*" We may only realize how when we look back at what we think is the beginning to try to find the answers. We all know about the proverbial "fork in the road", but do we always know it when we see it? Sometimes we do and make our choice, the right path or the wrong one, but not always. Sometimes, we only know it after it is past and, let's face it, we can't undo the past. Fortunately, God is a God of second chances.

This is my story of second chances and the promise that God has given me.

1

Wake up number one?

We don't always know when we get our wake up call. I thought I had the call at about 10 years old but it wasn't real. Someone was leading me but she wasn't God. She was a woman who was a member of the church our family attended. My mother was sick a lot back then and she had arranged for a woman by the name of Mrs. Jones to bring my sister and me to church. This may sound like a disguise but I assure you her name was really Jones. Mrs. Jones had been a Roman Catholic who converted to Baptist. Looking back on it all now, I realize she may have been on a mission to save souls. My mother had wanted us to go to church but I don't think she had it in her mind for Mrs. Jones to save us. She just wanted us to go to church each Sunday. Mrs. Jones would whisper in my ear when the pastor gave the invitation to be baptized and tell me how I could save my sister. I was the oldest you see and she told me my sister would follow me if I gave my life to Jesus. She once asked me if I would push my little sister off the bench in heaven. If she were on the edge, would I shove her off and let her fall into hell? To this day, I can still see that image in my mind just as clearly as I did then. I joined the church soon after and, of course, Shirley followed me to the front of the church. She gave her life to Christ along with me just as Mrs. Jones said she would.

For some time after that, I read my new Bible. The church gave us both a lovely new Bible for joining the church. I'm not sure if churches still give newly saved members Bibles on the day they are baptized but they did back then. At least the Baptist churches did in those days. I would spend many hours reading my new Bible and praying for God to answer my little girl prayers. Once, in grade school, I got into some sort of childish encounter with another kid that led to my receiving blows. Not a fighter by nature, I responded by saying something about turning the other cheek. I had heard and read in ***Mathew 5:39 "But I say unto you, that ye resist not evil: but whosoever shall smite thee on thy right cheek, turn to him the other also."*** Therefore, that is exactly what I did. I turned my other cheek to her and I received another blow for my trouble. This experience did not give me any satisfaction and I did not receive the "spirit" I was looking for.

In fact, I had a disappointing experience with prayer back then as well. We had some close neighbors who lived on our block. One of the family members was sick and in the hospital dying. Her name was Butzie and she had been very kind to me and a true friend. She was so very sick and I loved her very much and didn't want anything to happen to her, so I prayed. I remember being down on my knees praying very hard that she not die. I made vows, pleas, and promises to God of what I would do if only God would save Butzie. Butzie died. I was angry with God for a while thinking how could he not save Butzie. She was so young, too young to die really. I got over it eventually as time passed but that would mark a definite change in how I saw and felt about God. After that experience, I went about my little girl life pretty much as other little girls did. My mother continued to be sick off and on as we three grew up.

Being the oldest of three children, I was born in November of 1950, my sister was next, 13 months younger, and our baby brother was about 6 years younger than I was. Our family was probably one or two steps above what some might call "the working poor". My dad worked at many jobs. For a time when I was very young, he worked at night, I believe, at the post office downtown. Later he worked at a creamery around the corner from where we lived. He used to bring home from work these odd industrial canisters of whipped cream and ice cream that were about to expire. However, mainly he was a shoemaker. He repaired shoes. It was the family business. I remember at least two locations and heard of more shop locations he rented over the years. Daddy preferred working for himself rather than working for others. I am tempted, because of the relationship we had, to attribute this fact to some flaw in his character but that would be unfair since there is absolutely no proof of this. There is nothing in my memory to lead me there except that he had a very bad temper at home.

Daddy was not involved in the religious aspect of our lives. My dad had a Catholic upbringing and all of my relatives on my dad's side were Catholic. Mother grew up in the country and was raised a Baptist. She came from a rural part of the panhandle of Florida. I still have fond memories of our summers there and going to the little country church not far from my grandmother's house. Our family was very active in this little country church. My uncle George, Mother's brother, was a deacon I think and others had various duties within the little church that made it seem to me that our family had some influence there. Uncle George remained single until after my grandmother died. He lived with her, shouldered the responsibility of her wellbeing, and was her main financial support. She was my rock. Mama, as we called her, was the most stable adult in my life and the most spiritually minded person I have ever known. She was a loving, tender and understanding grandmother. She loved me like no one else. When she put her arms around me, I felt safe and loved. I can say, without doubt, God touched her. You could see it in her face.

Summers in Florida were what we looked forward to all year long. I lived for those few weeks each year. Most of my religious upbringing was there. We attended church every Sunday for Sunday school and morning services; we went to evening services and Wednesday night prayer meetings too. Some summers we went to vacation Bible school and "sings" or revivals. Life was full of opportunities for me to come to know God. However, it didn't really take. All I ever got out of it was, if you are good, you go to heaven and if you are bad, you go to hell. I knew a few Bible stories, I could name the books of the bible and I learned some of the most memorable gospel songs ever written.

By the time I was sixteen, I had seen many churches in a number of religions. Searching for a place I could worship God with all of my heart, soul, mind and strength, I found almost all of these churches within all the various religions I had explored had a plague. What plague? They had the plague of hypocrisy. The religions of the world all say theirs is the only way to God. If you are not in their religion, you will not go to heaven. Churches, or many of them, have the same plague with the added elements of false pride and arrogance. This arrogance is manifest in almost every church I have ever visited. Usually, you can see examples of it in the front pews. The hierarchy of the church generally inhabit those pews. The few, sitting with their cliques, would behave much like peacocks preening in their finery each Sunday as if superior to the rest of the flock. These cliques seem to feel they are better somehow than the rest of the congregation. They look at the rest of the members as less than or somehow poorer than they are. I saw them parade in on Sunday mornings dressed in their finery with noses in the air. They sat in the same pews each week with an air of superiority and haughty arrogance, piety oozing from every pore. Did they think they were better than the rest of us lowly parishioners? My experience with this attitude of the few had caused me to stumble over the years and driven me from many church congregations. Nevertheless, by the time I was a teenager, I was looking for something more exciting and hormone driven.

At the tender age of sixteen I was beginning to think I was going to be an "old maid". I know how this sounds now but, at the time, it was all too serious. It was ridiculous of me to think that way but all of the other girls had dates when I had not even a prospect of a date. Some of the other girls were going "steady" as we used to say. I didn't have a boyfriend, wasn't even dating anyone. It seemed as though I had two heads or something. Boys found me laughable, not dating material. I could count on one hand how many actual dates I had been on and still have fingers left over. My single status was the bane of my existence, or so I thought, and made me the butt of jokes in school. So lonely, I cried bitterly while listening to all of the sad teenage songs playing on the radio. It seemed I would never find anyone to share my life with or find my one true love. It is strange what a 16 year old thinks of. How did I get the idea that 16 was "over the hill"? Anyway, I did. It was the summer of 1967, the summer of love. We didn't call it that until much later but it would become known as that for good or for ill.

I was working part time at DH Holmes downtown on Canal Street that spring. The company, a New Orleans original, would close every weekend for a month in the spring and get teenagers to come in and count inventory. With the store empty, the escalators silent and unmoving, we would quietly invade every department. I was one of many who counted every scrap of everything in the store. We would go from department to department, count the stock, even the office supplies so that the store could know what was there, and what needed to be re-ordered. I counted shoes, underwear, buttons, cellophane tape even pencils. Boring isn't the word for counting inventory but it paid money and a 16 year old girl could sure use some extra cash.

This particular day, I was downtown finishing the last day of inventory. I had decided to stop by Woolworth's on Canal Street for an ice cream at the soda fountain. When I sat down, I noticed a familiar face. A girl I had just met a few weeks before was waiting on customers. For the life of me, I could not remember her name. I had met her at the 25th anniversary party for "Aunt" Horty Mae and Uncle Tony. "Aunt" Horty Mae was my mother's first cousin. We called her "Aunt" because she was so much older than we were. Horty Mae is a country name I have never heard anyone else ever called. Her mother was one of my grandfather's sisters. Anyway, this girl was the girlfriend of my Cousin Charles' best friend Tommy. Charles is one of Aunt Horty Mae's sons. A table had been set up at the party for the teens. My cousin Charles, his girlfriend Carol, his best friend Tommy and Tommy's girlfriend were at this table and I joined them there. That is how I met Ann. Her name was Ann or really Glenda Ann Davis to be precise. Most people called her Ann.

Ann and her mother Gloria were working together at the drug store that day. After I sat down, Ann noticed me and recognized me too. She came over with a smile of recognition on her face that seemed to say she was happy to see me. We began to talk about the party where we met and what I was doing downtown alone. I told her about my job and all the while, I was trying to remember her name. She knew mine but it was awful that I couldn't remember hers. Finally, her mother called to her for help and said her name, Ann. Whew, saved at last. She and her mother hustled around waiting on the customers at the islands and I watched thinking how experienced they both were at their jobs. I could also tell they weren't very happy with the work. They both looked tired and worn down by it all. No smiles, just tense expressions of frustration as they went about the tasks necessary to take orders of food and deliver them to the appropriate customers. I felt sorry for them. Finally, Ann had a few moments and asked if I would like to exchange phone numbers so that we could talk. I said yes. This was one of the most important moments of my life. It was a fork in the road for me that would lead directly to my NOT being an "old maid". *Was that you GOD?*

Ann and I began a budding friendship that evening that lead us to spend hours talking about our lives. We talked about our likes and dislikes; I shared with her my adoration of Elvis and his music. I told her of the many albums of his that I had, some of which I bought with the money I had earned at DH Holmes. We talked of boys and dating and I shared with her the fact that I didn't have a boyfriend but wanted one desperately. She told me she had four brothers. Whoa.....four brothers!! "How old are they?" I asked. She said she was the middle child of five with two older brothers and two younger. Naturally, I wasn't interested in the younger ones but the two older brothers were something I wanted to know more about. What could she tell me about those two? "Well, George is the good-looking one" she said. He was the younger of the two. All the girls were crazy about him. Oh how exciting this was but then she told me he was married. "Oh" I said, "well, what about the other one?" "Well," she said, "he's 21." Oh, that was older than I expected, I thought that wasn't good. I was 16. A 21 year old was a man, not a boy. The thought was a bit scary but I pressed on. I asked what he looked like. She said he was OK. Then she paused and thought for a moment and said, "Some people think he looks like Elvis." Oh my, be still my beating heart. Could that be for real? Did she really say that? Oh yes, she did.

We spoke again a few days later. She said her brother was visiting and asked me to come the next day and visit her at her house. I said I would. Then, she put him on the phone. His name was Gary. I was very nervous speaking to him for the first time. I babbled and acted like an idiot saying things I had never said before in an effort to impress a man but doing it badly. I do not remember the words; mercifully, my memory has erased them. However, I later learned that he definitely did not want to meet me. The thought of dating a sixteen-year-old girl was not what he wanted to do; after all, I was "jail bait". The next day, I dressed for success. I wore my sleeveless white, button up the front, button down collar, cotton blouse, a pair of white mid-thigh shorts and white tennis shoes and socks. If I have to say so myself, I looked good, I looked very good. Anyone who knew me would know I was sixteen, but no one else would guess. I looked every bit like a nineteen year old. I was tall, had been for years, and, since I never wanted to be a child anyway, I had practiced long hours at walking in high heels, talking and acting grown up. All of my young life I had felt odd, as if I were an adult trapped in the body of a child. I loved being around adults and listening to adult conversations. When younger, it was hard for me to associate with children of my own age or play children's games, I did not understand them and caused me to be even more isolated. I cannot explain why I felt this way only that it was true. I never wanted to be a child.

My makeup applying skills, developed with continuing practice were, in my mind, second-to-none. I studied up on these using the latest fashion magazines. My biggest problem with the way I looked was my hair. It was too curly. No, it wasn't just curly, it was frizzy. It took a massive effort, using every conceivable trick of hair gel and rollers and hair spray (extra, super hold) to tame what was on my head into anything resembling a normal hairdo. Shirley and I had the worst possible hair for our day. Over the years, we had both tried all sorts of remedies to fix our ugly hair. We even went so far as to purchase a product that was a horrible smelling pink goop, which was the hair straightener of our day. We spent long hours combing this junk into our hair trying to tame the kink out of our unruly locks.

When the results were less than satisfactory, we could not just give up. We continued by trying the conventional methods with limited success. The trick was to get the absolute biggest hair rollers on the market, the strongest holding hair gel and use it by the cupful. Once this was applied, put as many of those big rollers as possible on your head and get under the hair dryer for maybe 2 hours or until the gel was completely dry and stiff enough to crack. Ahhh, perfection!! Now, all we need do is to coax this stiff mess into something approaching what was the style of the day. But, as nice as it might look when finished, if one whiff of moisture, i.e. humidity, were to come near the finished coif, all would be lost. The humidity would turn the whole head of meticulously managed arrangement into the naturally frizzy mess it actually was. Living in New Orleans, where humidity rates can reach as high as 100%, was certain death for curly hair.

The *in* fashion of the 1960's was the long, straight, California girl look. Shirley and I had not gotten into the whole hippie movement; in fact, we barely knew about it. I wouldn't know the extent of this life style until much later. But until then, all we cared about was the clothes, makeup and hair styles. We tried to keep up with the fashion style but not the movement that went with it. The 60's style seemed to work against us.

As I dressed that day to meet this man, I thought about where I was going and how to get there. I wasn't used to riding public transportation. Our parents, or I should say my mother, made sure we didn't do a lot of traveling on public transit. As small children, our parents drove us everywhere we went. Only recently did we have limited access to the privilege of riding the streetcars or buses. I was nervous thinking of this today. Because, you see, for much more than just the bus ride, I was also going to the projects. Ann and her family lived in the new part of the St. Thomas public housing project. The new part was widely considered the more dangerous part of the St. Thomas public housing projects in New Orleans. Today, unfortunately, public housing projects are all much worse.

My mother had once lived in the old St. Thomas before meeting my dad and their getting married.

When she first came to New Orleans to work, she shared an apartment with an elderly woman. In the 40's, after the war, many country girls came from their small towns to find work and my mother did the same. Jobs were scarce in Altha, Florida and since Aunt Horty Mae was already here, she helped pave the way for Mother. When I was very little, Aunt Horty Mae's mother, Aunt Maude and her youngest daughter, Loretta, had lived in the old St. Thomas. They shared the little apartment with Aunt Maude tending as best she could while Loretta worked at some sort of office job. Loretta was a bit simple minded but able to work. She never married and after they left the projects, she moved in with Aunt Horty Mae. Aunt Maude's poor health would eventually lead her to a nursing home. Before that happened though, I can remember many times visiting Aunt Maude there. I thought the little apartments were lovely with their wooden parquet floors and newly painted walls. The apartment buildings were built out of what we in New Orleans termed "old red brick" with landscaping that always reminded me of Audubon Park. It seemed to me as if these lovely apartments had been put into a park-like setting. The buildings were amongst the stately old oaks of the city with Ligustrum and Azalea bushes and had manicured lawns that surrounded each building, not so the new section. These newer apartments were more like hastily put together matchboxes. In the new section it seemed any vegetation the city tried to establish died before its time. The trees, shrubs, grass all seemed withered, pale green or yellowed and brown. Dust devils picked up in the breezes that came from the river. In order to get to the apartment, I took the Jackson Avenue bus to the river and walked to the building that was theirs. Nervously, I took the stairs to the third floor dwelling. My heart pounded in my ears and my excitement was hard to contain as I approached the apartment. I didn't know for sure if the brother I spoke to the evening before would be there but that was all I could think about as I approached the door and waited to see what was on the other side.

2

Love At First Sight

Nothing in my experience was to prepare me for the adventure that began when I met the man who was to become my husband. As I walked into the apartment, I saw him for the first time. He had brown hair and brown eyes; he was 6 feet tall and weighed 200 lbs. Dressed in a white nylon shirt and dark pants, he was a bit rumpled. I found out he had fallen asleep and missed going in to work the night before. His mother, Gloria, had called in to say he was sick.

Ann introduced me again to her mom Gloria,

then to her brother Gary, her sister-in-law Mary and her little niece Lisa. Lisa was Mary and George's little baby who had just had her first birthday. As I write these words, I am trying to remember as many details as possible of the apartment and the people there but try as I might all of the details are a blur except one, Gary. I don't know what clothes they were wearing, the color of the floors or walls, the furniture or anything else about this scene. Most of what happened that day has been lost in time. The many years of living since has washed all but the most important fragments of time from my memory. I'll tell you what I do remember. I remember a lonely, sweet, sensitive young man who said he was tired of playing the game. When he spoke of his loneliness, it touched my heart and I knew what he meant. He wanted someone to share his life, someone sweet and kind that he could love. I felt the same except I hadn't ever played the game he spoke of, didn't know anything about adult games. At 16, what did I know about the games people play and how they could hurt each other? He had been hurt; you could see it on his face. At some point we were left alone with little Lisa who was our only chaperone. We sat side by side with Lisa between us and talked. I could feel the closeness of his body and, when he leaned in, it wasn't a surprise when he kissed me. I hadn't been kissed but a couple of times by a couple of different boys at this point in my life. Each one was less than what I expected from a kiss. One was so revolting that I ran from the boy in disgust. In the movies, you hear music during the kissing scenes but not so in real life. Bells should ring and trumpets should sound but not in my experience. Up until that point, kissing had been less than memorable. I can tell you, when he kissed me, I felt it. It was electric. Moreover, I will tell you something else, if he were to kiss me today the way he kissed me that day, I would get that same electric thrill. Gary is without a doubt a master kisser. He knows exactly how to kiss and put every ounce of passion and tenderness possible in a kiss. Wow, is he good, young or old, he is the best.

His being there that day to meet me got him into a bit of trouble with his current boss at Larry & Katz. Leo wasn't happy about his missing work the night before. Apparently, his job as a bartender was demanding. He hadn't had any time off for a long while and when it came time for him to go in to work the night before, Gloria had decided to let him continue sleeping and hadn't woke him up. That is why he was still there when I arrived. He worked at Larry & Katz seven days a week from mid-night to 9 AM. He and his brother had gone fishing the day before, had come back late in the day and he had fallen asleep at Gloria's. She decided to let him sleep instead of waking him to go into work.

Larry & Katz was a bar. The kind of bar that doesn't exist anymore. It wasn't for women, in fact, women had to have an escort and were not admitted without one. It was a man's kind of place. They didn't serve food and there were no tables or chairs only an old pool table and the bar area was a literal BAR. The main source of business was wholesale liquor sold to other businesses but they served hard liquor, mixed drinks and beer as well. There were even spittoons on the floor in front of the bar. It was located a block from Canal St. near the old Charity Hospital in New Orleans and served men at all hours of the day and night since they never closed. Men from cops to lawyers, from interns to doctors, newspapermen to journalists and TV reporters all of these and more could be found at Larry & Katz.

They called him Junior. He was the youngest member of the cast of characters who inhabited Larry & Katz. He worked the night shift and his job included stocking the bar, cleaning out the beer box, waiting on customers and mixing their drinks, taking out the trash and hosing down the sidewalks after a hard night of drinking. Add to all of these he also was a sometime bouncer when the need arose. At around 1 AM the band members from the various hotels and clubs in the Quarter would show up and unwind from a hard night of entertaining. Some of the entertainers from the My Oh My might be seen as well. The My Oh My was a club that had transvestite acts as its source of entertainment and the "girls" were sometimes so realistic as to fool those who didn't know where these fellows came from. Regulars to Larry & Katz knew to avoid the "girls" who came in with the owners of the My Oh My.

Thus, Gary was "Junior" to his fellow workers and the regular customers. He was the bartender. His job was hard but he liked it. He once told me he enjoyed this job more than any he had ever had. His main complaint was the midnight to nine in the morning hours. He would leave at 9 AM exhausted but still loved what he did. This seven day a week schedule didn't leave any time for dating. No time off! The others there loved to kid Junior, especially about his hair. He had a way, back then, of combing his hair. First, he would comb his hair to the back making sure the top and sides were neat, then he would use three fingers of his right hand and pull the hair at the center of his forehead down into a wave that resembled a slight curl. The guys at work would ask him to show them how he combed his hair then watch with mocking amusement as he would comb until it was just right. If he had to start over, the guys would say, "Oops, that wasn't just right, huh Junior, had to do it over?" and the laughter would erupt all round. He took this good-natured teasing as comradeship. They liked Junior and their teasing showed that they did. I am certain there is a whole book of fascinating stories he could write about his time at Larry & Katz's bar.

3

Gary and Me

That Wednesday, May 31st 1967, started a whirlwind explosion of excitement that turned my life of lonely, boring, colorlessness into a summer of love filled with explosions of color and passion that rivaled any movie I had ever seen, much less imagined. My summer of love began the day we met. How ironic that years later someone, somewhere would coin the term "Summer of Love" for the summer of 1967. We were just two people who found each other and felt the earth move. No hippie movement could match what we felt. No drug could bring us to a higher plain than the one we had found.

He walked me to the bus stop and when we parted that first day, we kissed and set a date for the following afternoon to go to the movies.

I had to start my summer with summer school classes the following week. I was not a good student. I had already failed the 5th grade a few years before. Through no fault of my own, or so I would tell myself, I had flunked out. It was the year I broke my arm. Shirley and I had been playing, she on her bike and I with my skates. She would ride up the sidewalk toward me and, as pre-arranged, I would catch hold of the back of the bike and ride along behind. We had been playing this little game for some time when, unbeknownst to me, Shirley decided she didn't want me to catch hold of the bike. I didn't realize she was going faster, too fast for me to safely grab the back of the bike this time. As I reached for the back rack, stepping off the grass and onto the smooth pavement, her speed propelled me from the grass onto the sidewalk and I lost my balance and my grip. I landed on my left arm at just the right angle to snap it just above the wrist. The accident ended our little game and we walked back home immediately. In all fairness, what happened next was a combination of my own hypochondria and my mother's impatience with it. You see, when we got back home and told Mother what had happened, she thought I was all right and didn't need to see a doctor. She didn't see fit to have my arm x-rayed either and I was told I would be fine and went on with my daily routine. I complained about my arm daily but mother ignored me. Some weeks later, Aunt Maude was visiting us and I was complaining of the pain in my arm. She took hold of it and proclaimed to my mother, "Elner, this child's arm looks like a green persimmon break". As I now understand it, a green persimmon break refers to the way a limb on a persimmon tree looks when it is broken and grows back crooked. The upshot of this was that I went into the hospital and, under anesthesia, my arm was re-broken and set in a cast. I missed some time at school and my teacher was kinder than she should have been. I didn't like doing school work, I got tons of attention that I definitely loved but, after milking this whole affair for all the sympathy I could, my grades suffered irreparable harm and I flunked the fifth grade. Of course it wasn't my fault, I had a great excuse, I had a broken arm and it hurt a lot. I had missed a lot of time while I was in the hospital, my arm was in a cast a long time and I just couldn't concentrate. Wasn't that enough? Would you like any more excuses? I could probably think of a few more if I took a little longer to think about it but why bother. I just didn't care enough to put forth the effort to do the work. In any case, I couldn't afford to fail another year.

Summer school was my only solution. Ugh! It wasn't like I didn't have the brains, I did. I just found school boring. There wasn't anything interesting about learning history from a timeline. I loved history normally but this years' teacher wasn't into history's "stories" only in the "timeline" of history. Just memorize what, where and when, that is all. As for math, it was not my forte and those two subjects were necessary in order to go on to the 11th grade.

I had left Prytania Private the year before to begin the 10th grade at Fortier High School. You might remember I said earlier that we were not very affluent so why would we be going to a private school? In the early 60's, southern schools were forced into being integrated. The federal government decided white families who were unable to afford private school tuition needed help in the form of subsidies. We fell into that category and my parents didn't want their children going to an integrated school so they applied for, and received, vouchers for us to go to one of the many newly established private schools that stepped in to fill the void. Prytania Private was in an old, Garden District mansion. Most of the students were from wealthy families but a number of us were the voucher kids. I did learn what the other side of the tracks looked like which taught me a great deal about the social order of things but as for actual knowledge, I probably learned as much there as I would have anywhere else. The rich kids were snobs and again I found myself around people who thought they were better than me. What a surprise! We spent four years there. I began in the 6th grade the year following my second year in the 5th and I left there after my 9th grade year. I was in class when we heard the news that President Kennedy was shot and killed in Dallas. That was my first experience with the "I'll never forget where I was when" moment. Much of the school erupted into chaos as the news of the shooting spread from classroom to classroom. Teachers and students leaving their classrooms began milling around the halls and I saw many of them crying or, at the least, having disturbed looks on their faces. A very wealthy girl I had classes with and I were the only two who were not acting this way. She was not a friend of mine however, we did speak this day about what we were experiencing. It is the only real conversation I can remember having with Avra. She and I both expressed confusion about why everyone was so very upset. What had happened was a horrible thing but we didn't understand the tears for a man none of them actually knew. In today's world I can only imagine what would happen if a sitting President, particularly the one we have now, were to be assassinated. I can see every school in the country having grief counselors bussed in for every school in the country to handle the profound effect the death would have on our communities. Before I would leave Prytania School I would have another one of those unforgettable moments, Hurricane Betsy would blow through and change our lives in another way.

Betsy was one of the worst hurricanes to hit our

area in a long time and even though our house wasn't damaged (we lost a few shingles) we did loose electrical power and had to boil our water for fear of contamination. I remember talk of Daddy and Uncle Mike going to the icehouse and standing in line for ice to put in our fridge and freezer to help keep the food from spoiling. My mother was practically cooking around the clock in an effort to salvage the thawed food we had in the house. It really hit home the old adage "waste not, want not" after Betsy. Mother was a country girl and had learned food storage but when your freezer is full of bulk vegetables you thought you had stored for the winter, you will need to scramble to cook or can them instead. We were without electricity for about 2 weeks so we all worked to either cook and eat or can as much as possible the rest of this food.

Everyone we knew was having the same problem. When we finally went back to school we began learning what others had gone through. I remember one girl in my class had lost all of her clothes, her textbooks, well everything she had really. Barbara was her name and she told of how the waterline inside her house was 2 inches below the ceiling. She lived in St. Bernard. Barbara had come back to school without books and wearing borrowed clothes because her family had lost everything. Those are the things you never forget.

I hated Fortier, it was big, impersonal and filled with kids I did not know and who did not want to know me. As much as I was out of my element at Prytania, it seems I didn't fit in here either. I kept to myself and drifted through that first year much the same as I had at Prytania only now I had to go to summer school in order not to fail another year of school.

I had not been looking forward to a summer of boring classes devoted to study, but now all of that had changed. Here was this fantastic new element suddenly changing everything. I had a date. Me, a date and with the most exciting person I had ever met. We were going to the movies. I couldn't believe it, should I pinch myself to see if it was a dream? I couldn't wait to get ready before he came to pick me up. My only concern was my mother. What would she say when she saw how old this guy was? Would she forbid this relationship? Would she stroke out? What would Daddy say? Would he hit the roof? He did have a vicious temper and could throw a fit at the drop of a hat. He could be totally irrational at times and you never knew what would set him off. I came to think of these outbursts as him just being a crazy *dago*.

My natural inclination is to see patterns. The pattern I saw in my dad was like many Italian men, domineering, selfish, macho bullies that treat women as slaves to their every whim. My daddy bullied us all. Most of all, he bullied my mother. She was his slave to cook his meals, clean his clothes and wait on him hand and foot. He didn't take much of an interest in us, the kids, but every now and then he would blow up and we never knew what he would decide to be angry about. I was glad my date would be arriving when Daddy was not around. At some point, he would still need to know about this new person I had met and I was worried about it but, for now, I was grateful that it could wait.

It is funny how thinking about those times brings back old memories that I haven't thought about for decades. Old folks used to talk of going down memory's lane and we would wonder what in the world they meant. I could easily get off track and wind up in another place entirely. For instance, I could tell you how Daddy treated me, how he treated Mother, how he favored my sister or how he raised my brother to be just like him. I could tell you how he called me stupid but, somehow, I think this would lead to a place that I do not want to go so I will just say he and I didn't get along at all.

Gary showed up at our door that day at exactly the time he said he would. He was always perfect at being on time. Maybe it's the German in him. When I met him, I thought his name would be the same as his sister. I didn't know then that they were half brother and sister. He and his brother George were from his mother's first marriage. Ann and her two younger brothers were from the second. When we had met the day before, he told me his name. He said it was "Hapenstringer" and he was German. I, of course, am Italian on my dad's side, Sicilian actually. In fact, my grandfather came to this country from Corleone, Sicily. On Mother's side we are Irish, English, Scottish and are rumored to have some Jewish by the name of Levi way back in time. To say that our children are a mixed up batch would be an understatement. My point in all of this is that Gary didn't even know his own name. Why? Because, his grandmother, the person who really raised him, did not know how to pronounce the name *Hab-is-write-in-ger*. His grandmother raised Gary and his brother when his mother dropped them off before running away with her second husband. They met their father on a bus one day when their dad overheard them talking and figured out these two boys were his own sons. It is a very sad story that I will leave for another time. Needless to say, as soon as I saw it written for the first time, I set about teaching him to pronounce this fantastic name. You see, I love this name. To me it is unique. Nobody else has a name like that unless related, of course. It stands out. I liked that and I was used to having a unique last name. Governale was mine. I hated my first name because it was so common. Linda. It was the "Lisa" of the fifties. In my second fifth grade class, there were five of us girls named Linda. How ordinary. I much preferred my middle name, Annette. After all, who didn't know

Annette Funicello? She was every boy's dream girl, right? I did love the boys. However, like I said before, they didn't like me much and certainly didn't want to date me. So, here I am answering the door to my future and, who steps in? Oh, my goodness, he did look like "Elvis"! He had changed. It was the same person but better. He'd had a bath, shaved and was wearing a baby blue oxford shirt, tight white jeans and some sexy, black "Tom McCann" shoes. He had combed his hair into that sexy wave in the front unlike the unkempt way it was the day before. Boy, oh boy, I had hit the jackpot. The man who walked through our door was passionate, gorgeous and not a bit of conceit, well maybe a tiny smidge of conceit. Did I mention the muscular build? Wow, his "V" shaped body was the icing on the cake that I had not seen the day before. He was not the dream for my parents that he was for me. The two things he didn't have were an education and a good job. So, we began our getting to know each other phase.

That summer we dated nearly every day. He worked at night, I went to school in the mornings while he got a little sleep, then he would pick me up at school and we would ride the bus to Canal Street for a meal and a movie. Sometimes he would be able to convince his brother to loan him his car and we would go to the beach. Pontchartrain Beach was the name of an amusement park at the lake. It was the place to go for kids. He didn't have a car so mostly we rode buses or the streetcar and I learned more about public transit that summer than I had in all of my life.

After meeting Ann, Gloria, Mary and Lisa I met his brother, George and his two younger half-brothers Greg and Glenn but the most important person in his life, the one who mattered most, was Grandma. She was the matriarch of the family. "Alberta Seibold Brink Hammond" was Grandma. If she did not like you, you were in trouble. No girl Gary or George brought home had ever passed the Grandma test. I was the first. She had run off every other girl either of them had brought into the house. For some reason, she found all of the other girls unsuitable. She could be just as harsh with their male friends as well. Gary would tell stories of how Grandma expressed herself about this friend or that even to their faces. She was a real pistol and she didn't care who heard it. I was different for some reason. She loved me until the day she died and I loved her. That is not to say I didn't have a healthy fear of her though.

Alberta was a force that must be reckoned with and the whole family knew it. Pure German, hardworking, dominating and outspoken, either she liked you or she didn't and she wasn't shy about saying so. No woman I have ever met has had so much grit as Grandma. She was the very definition of "True Grit". Born April 1st 1906, she was one of three daughters in the Seibold family. She was tiny, little more than 5 feet tall but not by much and when I met her she was like a little bull dog. She worked hard all day tending and cleaning the large rooming house she rented at 1325 Prytania Street. Her tenants were usually down on their luck men who had no homes or family, worked at odd jobs or for low wages and who could, on occasion be found passed out drunk. This kind of rooming house was very much like a flophouse in the old days. Alberta provided a service and she did her best with what she had. Gary,

Grandma and Maurice Hammond (Grandma's last husband) lived here. Maurice and Alberta had married some years before and Maurice was the only grandfather figure Gary and George had ever known. They called him Daddy-oh.

Daddy-oh was a big man. Together, Alberta and Hammond (she called him Hammond) made an odd-looking pair. She was so very short and stout; he was tall and barrel-chested with huge hands like vice grips. To look at them, you wouldn't know that there was an age difference. She was 61 and Hammond was 54. She kept her hair dyed in those days, preferring a deep shade of auburn red to her natural grey. He was grey and grizzled, belying his true age. It seemed to me he always had a day old stubble growth of gray beard similar to the way guys wear it on purpose today. His quiet strength was most clearly evidenced by the fact that he could take the cap off a bottle of beer or Coke and roll it up using only his thumb and fore finger. I'm not sure how familiar you are with the old bottle caps we had back then. The caps in those days were not the thin aluminum kind we have today but much thicker and made with what would be more like a tin can of green beans. The caps made in those days were lined with cork inserts; the cap was then crimped tightly around the edge of the bottle's top to keep it secure. We used a bottle opener to pry off the top. I have never seen anyone else roll a bottle cap as he did. Maurice was a very quiet man, solemn really. He did not talk most of the time. However, he did like to drink. His brand was Old Crow. Every evening after work, Grandma would allow Daddy-oh his daily bottle of Old Crow. Once he got home from work, he could no longer get into trouble and she could trust that no harm would come from his drinking. Otherwise, he would need watching like a hawk or he would get himself into serious trouble while drinking. The Old Crow would transform Daddy-oh into to a jolly version of himself. No longer solemn, he would joke and play with Gary and Grandma and the three became a lively trio teasing and laughing about times past. My privilege was to see these times for a short period that summer because Maurice was not long for this world. It is hard to believe, looking back, that just a couple of months later Maurice would be in the hospital and never make it back home. The two had gone on a vacation trip back to his hometown in North Carolina. When they returned he wasn't feeling well and was eventually admitted into the hospital. He passed away that August leaving Grandma desolate and lonely for the rest of her life. We all miss Maurice and Alberta and can only hope to see them again in the next life.

Gary and I began dating June 1, within two weeks he had given me his initial ring and ID bracelet to wear. These items were the tokens of going "steady" back then. Yes, I was going steady and approximately two weeks later, we became engaged when he brought me to Gordon's Jeweler's on Canal Street and told me to pick out my ring. I still think I have the best looking set of wedding rings of anyone I personally know. We both were so proud of the rings that we wanted to show them to everyone. This caused quite a stir in the projects. At dinner one night, as we sat around the table, Gloria and George began to berate Gary for buying such an expensive set of rings for me. He had used his charge account at Gordon's to purchase the $250 set of rings. The two of them were attacking him so viciously that I thought they would soon come to blows. This wasn't something I was used to seeing. There would be many things I saw that summer that were not a part of my experience. At some point, Gary's anger at this confrontation prompted him to explode and leave the room leaving me sitting there with the two of them glaring at me as if I were the reason for causing all this trouble. I remember saying to them both, "He's a grown man, and he's 21 and can do what he wants. After all, it is his money." Their reply was, "You don't know what you're talking about, why don't you just keep out of this!" I got up and went to see where Gary had gone. When I found him, I told him, maybe if it would keep the peace he should just take the rings back. When I tried handing him the rings, he flashed back, demanding that I never say that again and that I had better never take my rings off again either. The ring matter had been settled for now but, the tug of war had begun between them and me. This was now a family war, the sides were clearly drawn and Gary was firmly in the middle. I had no idea at that time where this would lead but this first battle would establish the tone of our family's relationships for the rest of our lives.

The summer was glorious once we were able to put aside the ring issue. We went to see movies, strolled through the amusements at the beach, swam in Lake Pontchartrain and went hunting, or I should say shooting, in Mandeville. We spent every moment possible together either alone or double dating with his friend, who was also named Gary, and his wife Margie. Gary was now burning his candle at both ends and wasn't getting any sleep, with work and dating, he couldn't keep this pace up so he lost his job at Larry & Katz.

His next job was driving a cab for the Yellow Cab Co. As you know, up until this time, Gary didn't have a car. Money was not the only reason for this. He had also lost his license sometime in the past for DUI's. He wasn't legal. I don't know why I am horrified at this realization now but I didn't see anything wrong with it back then. He applied and got another license by not telling the truth about losing his old license because of a DUI ticket. Until his little deception was uncovered, he was able to drive the cab for a while. He picked me up from school in his cab #556 and we were together even more.

A new school program was announced sometime that summer before my classes had ended. Offered though the public school system, it would train high school students to become practical nurses during their last two years of high school. It would consist of a half-day for required high school courses and the other half for nursing courses. In order to qualify, the interested student would need to go through a testing process. Since this was a new program, only a few students could participate and the selection process was in phases. Phase 1 was open to all those students about to start the 11th grade. It was like an open call audition with thousands of students competing for 30 spots. When I got out of Gary's cab that morning, it was a madhouse of kids from all over the city vying for these few openings to become nurses. We had to take one test after another during the entire day. I cannot remember if more than one day was required but it would not surprise me. I do remember having to stand in line for a time more than once so there could have been multiple days of this process. Once taken, the staff evaluated the tests, each student had an interview and told the results.

Some things we never forget. Where you were when this or that happened in history is common for us all as I have already said. This time however, I never forgot what I was told. My interviewer was the Director of Nursing herself. She was a thin, petite woman of about 40. Everything about her was crisp. I could see her in a nurse's uniform with the white shoes, white cap and white dress that was the custom of the day. Her hair was short, brown and slightly graying. She wore a reserved amount of makeup that could not hide the evidence of a time when she had had severe acne. She was very professional as she informed me of my scores. She knew I had needed to take summer school classes and wondered why I had done so poorly since my scores were extremely high. She told me my scores revealed I would do well in anything I choose to do. My potential was limitless, anything was possible for me. "Why do you to take this course", she asked. I told her I planned to marry in November and how I thought nursing would be a good trade to have. She agreed, I would be accepted into the program.

I could go on and on telling you of the summer

we had and believe me this could be a book all by itself, but that would take me down a path I don't think God wants me to go for now. I will just tell you we courted, I began the fall school season in a new school, took the nurses course, hated it, prepared for my wedding, had my 17th birthday on November 14th, got married the following week on the 20th and dropped out of the school and never returned. Whew... that didn't take long.

I was a married 17 year old dropout. Should I have gone on and become a nurse? Maybe. Would things have been different? Probably. Our life was not easy. We struggled with each other, we fought and we learned things the hard way, but we survived. We took the fork in the road that looked the easiest, but it soon became filled with rocks, ruts and huge potholes. We would both work at jobs a short while, quit, lie around the house for a while and get another crappy job only to quit again. We didn't have money for much but what we did have we wasted on foolish things like Christmas trees, Polaroid cameras and gifts for others. Marrying shortly before Christmas meant this would be our first Christmas together and

Christmas was supposed to be a fun time. Some if it was fun but our first gift-giving season was like crossing a mind field. One such incident occurred when we were preparing our gift list. We chose to purchase a new bike for my little brother. It didn't occur to us that we were doing anything wrong. When Gary's mother heard we had given my brother the bike, we found ourselves in a firestorm of monumental proportions. Gary had two young brothers that she felt he had slighted in favor of mine. We had definitely stepped on a mine with that decision. You just never know when you might innocently step on one and have it blow up in your face.

That first Christmas ended and we settled into the routine of a married couple. Our life back then was what I might easily call steamy. I can already feel my face getting red just remembering it. During that first year, sex was just about the only area of our marriage that we didn't have a problem in. But everything else was a mess. I didn't keep house well, we spent what money we had recklessly and couldn't find the self-control to keep our jobs for longer than a couple of months at a time. Simply put, we were children playing house without the discipline to be responsible for our actions. We needed to grow up.

My husband of less than a year was the one to take the next fork in the road of our lives together. He joined the U.S. Army to get away from me. Life was too hard with a child bride and the responsibilities that came with her, so he ran into the waiting arms of Uncle Sam. I cried as I watched him smiling and waving goodbye from the bus that would take him to boot camp. I would be going back home to Mother and Daddy.

4

Military Life

He soon realized this was not a safe haven from me. Camp was not the true emphasis of the term Boot Camp but the word boot was. He was now in the tender, loving arms of his Sergeant. His every waking moment would be filled with all manner of torture. He will tell you now that it made a man of him but I can tell you it wasn't long before I got the calls telling me how sorry he was he had left me. I wasn't having an easy time of it myself. My dad was worse than ever. He called my new husband every name in the book, told me he had left me, he was a bum, he would never come back and how I had ruined my life. Woe was he! My only escape was to get a job. I found one at Sears and Roebuck. Soon, I was making money to pay off our jewelry bill, my washer and dryer bill, our long distance phone bills. These were getting bigger and bigger. I was also spending a great deal on bus fare to Ft. Polk, Louisiana whenever I had permission to visit my husband.

Gary soon settled into the routine of basic training and the body fat that he had put on after our marriage began to melt. His body became one solid muscle and his endurance increased so that his reputation around the base was one of respect. He excelled at marksmanship and found his strength in all areas of the obstacle courses he was required to master. He was a good recruit. When I came for visits, we again became the united couple we were when we first met. We did love each other after all. He graduated after 6 weeks, I was as proud of him as I could be. In his uniform, he now looked like the Elvis of G I Blues. He was my "Soldier Boy".

During my time at home, I decided to go back to school at night to get my GED. It wasn't hard really. I passed all of the tests with ease, except for Math. It seems I had absorbed more than I thought as I scored at a college level in all areas but could only manage to reach the middle of the ninth grade in Math. I guess I stopped paying attention to Math in the ninth grade. It took me about a month to score high enough to take the test over and get my diploma. We had both begun to grow up a bit, but we were still a long way from being responsible. After boot camp, Gary got his orders. He was to go to Aberdeen Proving Grounds, Maryland for his A.I.T. training. He had leave during that Christmas, 1968 and left just after the first of the New Year to begin his next training assignment. I continued to work and save as much money as possible to prepare to go to Aberdeen when he got his next leave. I believe it was in either January or February when we packed up a few things, boarded a train, traveled to Aberdeen, Maryland, and again set up housekeeping together. This time it would be different. We had learned our lesson, right? We would do better, right? No, in fact, it got much worse. We nearly starved. After finding a furnished apartment we would live in, we had absolutely no money left for anything. Rent in Aberdeen Maryland, just outside of Washington, DC, was much higher than at home and food costs were higher in the East as well. We didn't have a car so we were stuck in the little base town. We couldn't even travel to D.C. and see the sights of our nation's capital. Our only form of entertainment was a radio and books.

The radio was of no use at all since all there was to listen to was news, news, and more news. Political news at that! We didn't have a TV but there was a rental shop that rented TV's by the month. After the first month, we scraped together the few dollars needed for a month of TV. I remember crying as we trudged through the snow to bring it back after our month was over. All we had left for us to keep our sanity was books. It is a good thing we both loved reading. We would go to the base library and grab armfuls of books, go home, crawl into bed side by side and read for hours.

Gary and I both lost a great deal of weight during this time but I looked the worse for it. There were times all we had to eat was grits with margarine or crackers and ketchup. I remember reusing tea bags more than once to stretch them and make them last. I even needed to visit a local food bank once. He did try to bring home food for me from the mess hall but still that was a hit and miss situation. In fact, at some point, that kinda backfired on me. I contracted mononucleosis as a result and was sick for a while. When we met, I was 5 feet 7 ½ inches tall and weighed 145 lbs. When we left Aberdeen, I weighed 123 lbs. Mother cried when she saw me. When I boarded the plane for the first flight of my life, the one thing I didn't realize I was bringing home was a baby.

It was the end of April 1969 and we were coming home on leave before Gary shipped out for his next duty station in Korea. He had a month of leave we used to get me set up and settled in. Before I realized I was pregnant, I found a job with Ma Bell. I was what then was called a *Special Assistance Operator*. In those days, if you dialed a number that was changed or no longer in service, you got someone like me. We worked at a long line of stations all connected to one another. We were located in a huge room with row after row of stations where we were taking calls from customers expecting to speak to their loved ones or some business or other. However, because the number had been changed or disconnected recently, they got one of us, the women of Ma Bell. It was Southern Bell Telephone Company. My station was a big board that was about 3 feet in height and approximately 2 feet wide with holes in it. Under each hole were lighted numbers to let you know the exchange the call was coming from. On the desk-like portion were flexible cords with funny looking ends that fit into the holes on the board. We wore headphones with a microphone to speak into when we answered calls. If you have ever seen the comic routine of **Lily Tomlin** playing **Ernestine**, you would know what this looked like. When a call came in, we would pick up a cord, plug it into the lighted hole, see the exchange then reach for the appropriate directory. New directories needed publishing every few days with the numbers that had been changed or disconnected and we would use these to give the information to the people whose calls we answered. It was a nerve-racking experience. As special assistant operators our orders were to answer the call, give the correct information, end the call and take the next one in less than one minute. If you didn't do this quickly, a call could get dropped because they weren't passed automatically to another station as you might see today. I'm talking about 1969. Things were much different then, we didn't have computers, we were the computers. There were monitors behind us, women who were watching us and keeping track of our progress and how long we took to get to the next call. We didn't get breaks except for lunch or if we were on a split shift, no break because the split was hours long. I hated split shifts. When I started the job, I didn't know I was pregnant. As it turned out, my condition soon became an issue. I was so nervous I began to get sick, nauseated and was repeatedly asking the monitor to go to the bathroom. Because my behavior was not in keeping with the rules, I needed to see a doctor to see what was wrong with me. That is how I found out I was going to have a little bundle of joy. The only person who was happy about this was Gary. My parents were not happy, his family wasn't happy, I wasn't happy, Gary was on his way to Korea and I had just lost my job.

My parents still lived in the city at this time and New Orleans was changing. The anti-war movement was at its height, hippies had joined with the radicals and there were riots in the streets and at colleges around the country and the world. Our neighborhood had become a haven for drug dealers and it was nothing to see money changing hands and people shooting up in cars that would sometimes part in front of our home. Evidently, there were dealers nearby who chose our house occasionally for their meeting place. We had to move.

The house we called home was a double shotgun purchased during World War II by my dad and his brother Mike. A shotgun house is a house built with the rooms connected end to end from front to back. A double was two of these joined down the center, side by side. We lived on one side and my uncle and his family lived on the other. The decision was made the summer of '69 that we were moving to the 'burbs. Uncle Mike had already bought a new place in Metairie and we were on the hunt for a house out there as well. Finding a new home wasn't easy for my mother and dad but finally the best that could be afforded was found and now the fun began.

The paperwork had been finalized for the new

house in Metairie; the house on Josephine Street had been sold, but before we could move, Hurricane Camille took aim at the gulf coast. I had experienced Betsy and the aftermath of that storm, now it was Camille's turn. The most memorable part of this experience for me was being in the front bedroom lying on my parents' bed resting. With me was my little cousin Diane. Diane was Uncle Mike's daughter and she was probably about 10 or 11 years old at that time. We were lying in the bed because we were told to keep out of the way in a safe place. Since I was pregnant, and she was still a kid, we stayed there while the rest of the two families were trying to batten down the hatches. Our two families had decided to ride out the storm together that night. There was a lot of hustle and bustle going on around us not to mention the storm itself. As I was lying there, I noticed something strange going on with the ceiling above the bed. A few years before, Daddy had decided to lower the ceilings in the house. He had put in these Styrofoam looking panels. These white panels were about 3 feet long and about 1½ feet wide. Other panels were textured and clear plastic where florescent lights were the lighting for the room. These panels had been set into framework so that, if necessary, they could be lifted up and out to either change them or, in the case of the clear panels, the florescent bulbs could be replaced as needed. As I lay there, I noticed these clear panels. They would rise up and come down within the frames, as the wind would blow. I began to imagine what would happen if the wind were to get any stronger. I could see the possibility that one of these panels might actually come out of the frame and fall on Diane and me. I began to tell my mother and Diane's mother how concerned I was that this could happen. "No, no Linda, that can't happen. Stop being so paranoid, nothing is going to happen." I wasn't convinced and didn't stop my complaints. At some point, someone made the move for us. A rollaway bed was set up in the living-room. As soon as Diane and I were moved into the new bed, the panel that was suspended above the bed we had been in flew out of its frame and crashed into the bed sending a thousand pieces flying through the two rooms. Later, I found pieces of the panel in the bed we had been moved to. I don't want to think what might have happened had we not moved from that bed. Was that you God?

Camille would be one of many historic events that would take place that summer. Thinking back, so many unusual things happened both good and bad the year I was pregnant. Camille was a category 5 when it hit land, making it the only one in history to do so. That summer alone, many historical things happened but I only paid attention to two, the storm and the moon landing. Some other significant things that happened that year were Nixon took office, Elvis made his comeback, the Beatles' had a slow brake up and John & Yoko marry. Arafat becomes PLO leader, James Earl Ray confesses to shooting Dr. King and Sirhan Sirhan admits he killed RFK. Golda Meir becomes the first female prime minister of Israel, Ike dies, the SDS (Students for a Democratic Society) takes over Harvard and many are hurt and arrested. A little known teenager dies in St. Louis of an unknown disease and confirmed as the first North American HIV/AIDS victim. The SDS has its convention in Chicago and the radical Weathermen seize control of the organization. Judy Garland dies, the Stonewall riot in NYC is the start of the gay rights movement, the Zodiac Killer strikes again and Chappaquiddick hits the news when Kennedy drives off the bridge killing Mary Jo. Charlie Manson goes on his killing spree and then there is Woodstock, all of these and more happened in 1969. I am not sure there was another year like it.

My focus however, as I said, was on having a baby and I don't feel any shame in telling you I was scared. I had not wanted children in the first place, in fact, that was one of the first serious conversations Gary and I had when we began dating. Now that having a baby was a fact, I had no idea what to expect. Gary was in Korea for 13 months. I was here with my parents who needed to move from the city to the suburbs with a hurricane tearing up the gulf. We still had not packed a single box. The new owners were due to move in and no one was lifting a finger to get out of here.

One particular day I flipped out at both of my parents. I must have been a sight in front of my whole family yelling and screaming to the top of my lungs "We have to get out, don't you people get it?" "Are you all crazy? We don't own this house anymore!" Finally, somebody had gotten the ball rolling, we all pitched in, got it together and moved out. Honestly, to this day, I don't know why it took me losing it to get them to start packing up. The irony of it all is that the house I grew up in is still as solid as a rock but the house in Metairie is gone thanks to another killer hurricane, not Camille, but Katrina.

As the summer days turned into fall, I started to pick up weight. I started my pregnancy at 123 lbs. By the time I delivered my baby, I weighed 165 lbs. The summer heat was miserable but the new house had a wonderful back yard, something we didn't have in the city. I would go out on the carport to catch the breezes from the lake every afternoon and plan for when Gary would come home on leave. I planned every detail of his homecoming. Even though I wasn't working, I did receive my allotment from the Army and, using it wisely, I paid the few bills we had, bought an old car for $150 and found a way to get his driver's license back to finally make him legal to drive again. I had the surprise all planned. When he got off the plane, I would give him this little box gift wrapped with a set of keys sitting on top of a cotton square with his license underneath. He had no idea.

He came home in time for my 19th birthday and our second anniversary. Our baby was due on December 25. It would be a tight squeeze but babies don't usually arrive on their due date, I was hoping it would be early.

My doctor, in my opinion, was the best in the world. His name was Julius T. Davis, Jr. He had been my mother's OB/GYN when I was born and here he was for my baby and me. Dr. Davis was my Marcus Welby, MD. For those of you who don't know who Dr. Welby is, use Google or Bing and find out. Dr. Welby was played by Robert Young and he was just the best fictional TV doctor ever. I loved Dr. Davis and I trusted him. As the time approached for Gary to leave and I hadn't even begun to dilate, we decided to induce labor. On December 16, 1969 Rhonda was born and a week later, Gary left to return to finish his tour in Korea.

There is so much of this period I am skimming over, if I didn't, I would never finish. I could write another whole book on this period alone. One thing I'm not leaving out is how I didn't think about GOD. I am ashamed now at how little I thought of Him even at my most desperate times back then. I didn't see it and I certainly didn't deserve it but He was there with me the whole time. So many others had sorrows, the world was in turmoil, people were dying, evil was everywhere but I didn't even know it was happening. Don't get me wrong, I knew much of what happened back then but many of the stories I have previously listed went right by me. I was just too into my own world to notice.

My first priority once Gary left and I was back on my feet was to lose weight and get a job. Daddy was on me like white on rice. "That guy is a no good bum. He's left you and now you got a baby. Look at her, that's right, they're just alike, the both of them, two peas in a pod." This was the conversation round the kitchen table one night as Mother held her first grandchild, feeding her a bottle. Daddy had come home from work in a foul mood and I was sitting on the other side of the table watching as he let loose with another of his tirades. He had done so with such frequency that it had begun to lose its sting. I was stupid and I had married a bum. Now I had produced another one just like me. Wow, there was no pressure here. I had few people I could turn to with Gary away. My sister and I had our issues, besides she had her own life in the person of her soon to be husband, Charles. I will not go into this here but her marriage was to be no bed of roses either. My brother, self-centered as he was, had no interest in anything to do with us. Mother was my only friend. I hadn't kept up with any of the girls I went to school with, none of the people I had worked with were ever my friends, even my extended family on both sides were not available as confidants. This bothered me greatly. Why was I friendless? I loved people, I enjoyed being with other people and having a good time. I was outgoing and bright so why was friendship so hard for me to come by? This fact would haunt me for most of my adult life. My mother did take my side that night by saying she didn't see anything wrong with my baby and me being two peas in a pod. He hadn't meant anything good by what he had said, it was clearly meant as a slam and she and I could see it by the scowl on his face.

I had to get out of there and do something or I would lose my mind. The best way to appease Daddy was to get to work. I set about doing just that. I found a job working at a little furniture store on Magazine Street called Fisher Furniture. I mainly answered the phone and was the cashier but I sometimes did collection work on past due accounts. I liked the job but it wasn't much of a challenge intellectually. As it turned out, it was great for my physique. I hadn't learned to drive yet so I rode in to work with Daddy every morning.

His shoe shop was on Magazine Street. My dad was a shoemaker. He fixed shoes for a living. He and his brother Mike were both shoemakers who learned the trade from their father. Daddy was even a shoemaker in the Army, fixing shoes for the troops in World War II. We came into town each morning very early to beat the rush and Daddy could open early for his customers. We usually arrived by 7AM. In the beginning, I would sit in the shop until it was time for me to go in for 9. It only took me 15 or so minutes to walk the rest of the way from Daddy's shop to Fishers. Sitting in the shop for nearly 2 hours with Daddy every morning soon became torture. However, if I were to have him drop me off on the corner of St. Charles Avenue and Napoleon Avenue, I could take a nice long walk to work. Fortunately that spring, most days were beautiful and the walks were pleasant. This area of town is lovely and the smell of the old oaks reminded me of picnics in the park. It was safe in those days and I had no fear that anyone would harm me. The long walks not only trimmed pounds and inches off my hips but they gave me a break from Daddy's constant negativity. I had time to think and clear my head before work. This job allowed me to save as much as I could for the day when Gary would finally return and we could be together again. I would work hard and have an even better car for us this time.

God is good. After finding the $150 car I purchased for us before Rhonda was born, God let me find a $1500 car that was perfect for us to get to Gary's next duty station. I had found the car through an ad in the newspaper. A young hippy couple from up north was selling it. The little Volkswagen Squareback was in nearly perfect condition. The little, dark blue car was VW's version of a station wagon. The couple had taken good care of it with the exception of leaving strawberries in the back until they spoiled. They had a small baby who loved the strawberries they had purchased while visiting the *Ponchatoula Strawberry Festival* that year. Leaving the baby girl to her own devices in the back of the little blue car with the strawberries, she did what toddlers do. She mashed and squeezed those delightfully juicy berries to a pulp getting the juice all over her and imbedding them in the many crevices of the back of the car. Once there, the car would forever smell of musty strawberries especially in the heat of summer. Fortunately, I love the smell of strawberries. I had saved $500 so I took out a personal loan at our local bank for the rest of the money. The only drawback to the car was it was a standard transmission and I hadn't learned to drive a standard and never would. It is ironic. To this day, in our little family unit, I am the only one who has never learned to drive a standard.

Gary came home, in June of 1970, with orders for Ft. Hood in Texas. We packed up the VW with the most essential of our meager possessions along with Rhonda and drove to Texas. We headed into the next chapter of our lives with high spirits. Happy to be together again after 13 months, we had all the optimism in the world. With Rhonda, now 6 months old, in the back of the wagon, surrounded by everything we could fit into the little car, we drove to the little town of Copperas Cove. Copperas Cove was a neighboring town to Killeen, Texas the town that served as the support area for Ft. Hood. Killeen is the larger of the two and where most of the service men, who lived off post, would find apartments for themselves and their families. That summer, apartments and houses were scarce in Killeen, which is why we found ourselves in Copperas Cove. The only affordable, available place we could find was an old, two-bedroom house. It was in deplorable condition. There were open spaces around all the windows and doors, the furniture was cheap and falling apart, the fridge wasn't working and everywhere we looked, including the open fridge, there were dead roaches. The house had been sprayed for pests before we rented the place, but it hadn't been cleaned. That left us with the dirty job of getting rid of what looked like millions of roaches. The kitchen cabinets were the worst. We had to scoop them up with a dustpan and broom. All of the cabinets had them at least an inch thick, not even the refrigerator had been spared the infestation. We found them everywhere. After getting rid of every single dead carcass, we were constantly on the lookout for any more. I couldn't bear the thought that my baby would find one and try to put it in her mouth. I didn't let her crawl around the house. In fact, we kept her either in a playpen, high chair or her baby bed if we weren't holding her. With so many open crevices all over that house, there were a million ways for creeping, crawling things to get in.

We settled in and began his tour of duty with a great deal of promise. We had a car, a portable TV and many of the things given to us for our wedding that we could finally use. This was much better than the situation we had either after our wedding or in Aberdeen. Our first place after getting married was a shotgun house in the city. I wasn't a good housekeeper. No, that's not exactly accurate. I was hideous. Lazy wasn't my middle name, it was my only name. Washing dishes, dusting, sweeping and all of the other chores that make for decent living were not on my list of importance.

Gary and I both were terrible at being responsible with our money and our duty to each other. We were great at love making, period. We were as compatible as two people could be in that department. Our wedding night was all it should have been, but it didn't take long before the house became a pigsty. Dirty dishes, trash, dirty clothes and a lack of cleanliness were evident throughout the house. That was my job and I wasn't doing it. I went to work at a couple of places during this period but neither of them lasted long which meant I wasn't very good at that either. Gary too had a few jobs that year. He quickly lost them all when he would call in sick or just not show up. It was no wonder he ran off to the Army. If it had been me, I would have left me too! We were both so very young and irresponsible. We needed to grow up.

Our new home in Aberdeen started off being a better fit than the little house we began our marriage in or the little apartment in Aberdeen was but, became worse because of the isolation I felt now that we had a baby. I wasn't used to having to care for

Rhonda all by myself so the unkempt living conditions became pretty much the same or even worse, which proved I hadn't learned anything from my previous experience. I hadn't gotten any better. The few times I tried and got something done weren't enough to create a pattern of responsibility in me. Here we were again, only now there was a baby. Would I get better with this new opportunity? No, I was actually worse than ever. Gary was doing his job. He hated the military but he knew the consequences of not going to work. Uncle Sam wasn't as understanding or flexible as a civilian boss would be. You didn't get fired if you didn't show up. Bad things happen but being fired isn't one of them. He had learned to get up and go to work whether he felt like it or not. He has always said the military made a man of him. So far, it had not made a woman of me. We fought about the housework, money, the baby and pretty much everything. I was lonely, bored and felt afraid I would never be happy again. That's all I ever wanted, just to be happy. I had once said that to my nursing instructor. The one who interviewed me for the course I didn't finish. Before we got married, she pulled me aside and asked me why I was getting married. That is exactly what I told her, "I just want to be happy." She told me she had a dream about me. In her dream, she said I had come to her afraid and crying. She told me I didn't have to go through with the wedding. She was trying to warn me not to marry Gary. I know she cared about me and thought I was making a big mistake but I wasn't interested in anything she had to say on the subject. I loved him and that was that. I thought this would make me happy. If I knew then what I know now, I could have prevented so much suffering from ever happening.

We were in Texas for 19 months. We lived through one of the worst periods of our marriage. We abused each other terribly. There were fights and recriminations with each of us blaming the other for all of our ills. At one point, the fight culminated in my leaving with Rhonda and going home. I had left him. I think that lasted maybe two weeks but we talked it out and I came back.

Gary hated the Army but he reenlisted anyway. As his first enlistment got closer, he knew a reenlistment would come with a windfall. He would receive, in effect, a "signing bonus" of $10,000. That kind of money in 1971 was a tremendous carrot and an offer he could not refuse. I don't remember objecting since we had many uses for the money. He could also put in for his next assignment and chose Hawaii. While we waited, we traded our VW for a brand new gold Plymouth Duster, purchased a console color TV, a few new clothes, a new set of stainless steel pots and pans and a fancy sewing machine with a cabinet. Let's see, I still have the pots or most of them anyway. All the rest are gone. He didn't get Hawaii, instead, his first set of orders came for Germany, which he could refuse. We waited a bit longer and again he got Germany. This one we had to take. I believe we had a month to get things packed up and all of our arrangements made before he left the states. The military arranged for our things to be put into storage until we had base housing in Germany. Since he had made Corporal, I could go to Germany too. I would have to wait until base housing was available for my travel orders would come through. In the meantime, Rhonda and I were to return and stay with my parents. This stay would prove to be the most serious of all.

In January of 1972, Gary left for Germany and I moved back in with my parents. I expected to be there no more than a month or two. When that didn't happen, other more bizarre things did. Mardi Gras day proved to be a pivot point which came in the form of a toothache. I had gone to the parades that day to see George, Mary and Lisa ride on one of the truck floats. I ate some popcorn, a husk got lodged in a back tooth and the tooth became very sore. So sore in fact that I needed to see a dentist in order to get rid of that husk lodged somewhere in my back teeth. I didn't fear dentists. I had a great dentist as a child. Dr. Leggio on Magazine was my dad's dentist and he took me there as a child. There is still a Leggio dentist on Magazine Street today. One of my fondest memories as a child was of the praise Dr. Leggio gave me for being so brave in his chair. Another of his patients, a little girl, wasn't so brave. She and her brother would have their appointments before me each time we went. The brother would go in first and the sister last. He and I would go out and sit on the front porch of the old house that was the dentist's office. We listened to her screams as Dr. Leggio would clean her little teeth or fill a cavity. We laughed at the overreaction she had to each of her visits. My turn would come, I would climb up into the dental chair and Dr. Leggio would say, "See how good she is, why can't you be this good and not cry so much?" I have never feared any dentist especially after that.

I needed to find a new dentist and chose one close to the house in Metairie. He was able to remove the husk but told me I needed to have my wisdom teeth removed. The two bottom teeth would never break through my gums because the roots had wrapped around my jaw and the crown was facing out instead of up. After careful consideration and the advice of the dentist, I decided that I would use my *CHAMPUS* insurance, check into the hospital and have all four teeth removed at once. I won't bore you with the details but it was a big mistake. After I got out of the hospital, I got four dry sockets and pleurisy as a result. The pain and drugs, along with some disturbing letters from Gary resulted in my rethinking our marriage. What happened was I lost my mind. After weeks of pain and suffering, some strange letters and phone calls from Germany, I got a lawyer and asked for a divorce. Gary had gotten some bad advice from someone over in Germany who told him to use a few dubious phone calls to make me jealous which made things in my mind much worse. Ever since Texas, we had been on shaky ground and now it seemed our marriage was about to finally end.

I went back to work for the phone company but this time as directory assistance. I didn't like the work but it was money. This office was located in old Metairie and closer to the house than the office in the city was. The office building was on Metairie Road. Since the Duster was an automatic, I was finally able to get around but still didn't feel confident enough to drive into the city. I put Rhonda into day care and proceeded to try to make a new life without Gary. It was ok for a while but I did miss him. I felt like a fish out of water and even more alone. Believing I had made a bad marriage, I was afraid of ruining my own life and Rhonda's and destroying Gary's life as well. It was definitely a mess.

Gary came home on an emergency leave in June. We met at the airport, went to a motel room to hash things out, stayed the night and made up. We loved each other, there was nothing else to say about it. We used the time he had to do fun things and reconnect. He then returned to Germany, used what little money we had to get Rhonda and me a commercial flight to Germany and off we went. I had no idea what I would find when we got there but I was committed to a new beginning.

5

Germany and The Witnesses

We left New Orleans, landed in New York, took an Air France flight to Paris then on to Frankfurt in a small twin-engine jet. By the time we landed in Germany I felt as though I had gone through a meat grinder. Did I tell you Rhonda was hyperactive? No? Well, she was. While she was having the time of her life, I was beside myself trying to keep her from sitting in everyone's lap on the plane. I was never so happy to arrive anywhere in my life as I was in Frankfurt that day. Gary met us at the airport to drive us back to Butzbach, Germany. He was currently stationed there as part of the 3rd Armored

Division, also called "The Rock". He had arranged for us to stay in temporary housing with his Sergeant whose family was currently awaiting their permanent housing assignment as well.

Temporaries were apartments made available to dependents', the soldier's family, waiting for permanent housing. These apartments were located on the top floors of the buildings where the permanent housing apartments were. The American Government had constructed these buildings after World War II for use by American soldiers and their families. The apartments now used as temporaries were originally the "maids" quarters. Back then, the families that lived below had their own "maid" assigned to them. These women were hired by the military and housed in the same building as their charges. Each building's top floor had two "maid's" quarters, below each building, there were 12 regular apartments. Each housing area had many of these buildings and there were numerous housing areas located all over Germany at the various military bases.

Our sponsor, Sgt. Prevy and his wife Claudia, had

agreed to let us stay with them while we waited for our own temporary assignment. Since this was one of those former "maid's" quarters, as you walked in the front door, you saw a common living room, dining area, bathroom and kitchen area. The head "maid" had a larger bedroom. There was a long hallway lined with six smaller bedrooms. Finally, there was another bathroom at the end of the hallway and then the back exit that led to an outside staircase. Each bedroom had two twin sized beds and a dresser for each. I don't remember if there was a closet so there may not have been one in there. Last, but not least, there was a radiator for heating in each bedroom. These rooms were quite cold even in the summer. The average temperature around Frankfurt in the fall is 68°F. That is very different from the 90's we have in New Orleans not to mention the humidity. It was freezing in those apartments.

We were welcomed at first but soon the Sergeant and his family found our presence an intrusion. I admit that we could have been better guests but the one thing I was conscientious about was helping Claudia with cleaning, cooking and doing dishes.

Wanting to be a good guest and not make waves, I was taught to do these things. After an incident involving Rhonda where I was negligent, we decided to keep to ourselves at the opposite end of the apartment. Rhonda, as I said, was a hyperactive 3 year old who needed watching constantly. I hadn't done my job. I don't remember why now but for whatever reason I hadn't been watching her and she decided to create a work of art on the walls in the living room. I understood and felt badly about the trouble we had caused. I tried to clean the crayon marks from the wall but Claudia wasn't pleased. With the atmosphere so frosty it was best that we steered clear. After a couple of weeks at the other end of the apartment, it seemed Ms. Claudia was offended by my distance and picked a fight with me and we nearly came to blows. As you already know, I am not a fighter so we left the apartment choosing to take our things and leave rather than to continue arguing. Before I had come to Germany, Gary had purchased a used vehicle. This car was an old VW bug that had every part of it painted a different color. One fender was orange another was blue and so on for the doors and hood, etc. Leaving as we did still meant we did not have a place of our own so we all three spent the night in the forest nearby. You haven't lived until you sleep in a German forest. We three huddled together in blankets on the ground under the trees and awoke with stiff necks and sore backs.

The next morning, when Gary got to the base, all hell broke loose with Sgt. Prevy in serious hot water. He was, after all, Gary's sergeant and his sponsor. Gary was his responsibility. It wasn't seemly for us to be sleeping in the forest when he had taken the assignment to house us until we had our own quarters. The upshot of the whole incident was that I refused to return until Claudia backed off. With a little talking to, her husband persuaded her to apologize to me and we finished out our time there in the last bedroom of this weird apartment.

We finally received our housing orders and moved into our first apartment that fall but it was not in the same housing area. Instead, we had a temporary in a smaller housing area in the town of Wetzlar. I don't remember much about the town of Wetzlar itself. We didn't know anyone in this housing area when we got the assignment. It was located further away from the base and the housing area where Stg. Prevy and Claudia were. We were all alone, isolated from the main base and all of the resources that came with military life. When you are in the service and assigned to a foreign country, you are dependent on the military for food, clothing, shelter and medical aid. To address these, the U.S. military provides its personnel with housing areas, commissaries, the PX, dispensaries and hospitals. With housing met, we needed to find where the commissary was to get our groceries, the PX for clothing, hardware, gas and household supplies and the dispensary for minor medical needs. The closest hospital was 97th General in Frankfurt. Getting any of these needs met using the German "economy" was very expensive. Little things like fruit and vegetables maybe, but to see a German doctor or supply a home with the usual things, we would need to go to the PX (Post Exchange) or the dispensary for a doctor. As I said, we had a car and Gary was a great driver. Service members were required to pass a test to get a driver's license in order to drive in Germany. Gary only needed to take the international driver's license test two times to pass. Others took many tries to pass. I tried but that thing was ridiculous. In hindsight, maybe I should have gotten it since I was to be alone a great deal in the next few years. I could have been more independent had I gotten my international license. The Army has a saying, "If we had wanted you to have a wife, we would have issued you one." Gary belonged to the Army, not to me. He did what they told him to do, when they told him to and how they told him to do it period.

It wasn't long before Gary received his first field duty assignment since my arrival. This was to be my first experience at being truly alone in a foreign country. Field Duty simply meant going to the woods and playing war games. I use the term "playing" loosely. They played war games in Grafenwöhr a few times a year for 6 weeks at a time leaving wives and children behind. From what I understand, these games are all too real. They slosh around in the mud and snow with their guns and packs according to the tactics devised by the war gamers pretending to be in a war and trying to win. They have all of the same equipment they would have to fight a battle including the tanks and armored personnel carriers. Gary's job in the army, what they had trained him for, was as a welder. When he signed up, he was asked to pick an MOS or job he would like to do. His scores were very high on the army IQ tests and they told him he could pick anything he wanted except computers. He looked at all of the classes available, saw Heavy Equipment Diesel Mechanic, and reasoned this could be a good way to make a living when he got out. In typical Army fashion, when he got to AIT in Maryland, they put him into a class to learn a computer job called Aircraft Armortry. Once the mistake was realized by the brass, he again was given a list of available classes. Since they didn't teach diesel mechanic's at APG, he finally chose welding. He has been a welder ever since.

He was miserable in Grafenwöhr. He got filthy, had to sleep in a tent with a bunch of other filthy GI's and ate sea rations, no MRE's in those days. If I were to describe what I think it was like, I'd say watch "Band of Brothers" except without the Germans trying to kill them. At the same time, he worried if Rhonda and I were all right. Before he left that first time, I had gotten a terrible cold that settled in my chest. After he came home from work the evening before he deployed, we went to see a doctor at the dispensary who prescribed a strong cough medicine with codeine and told me to drink a German beer along with a dose of the medicine. We stopped on the way home that night, bought a few bottles of German beer and I dosed myself. By the time we got home, I was loaded. I sang zippidy doo da all the way up the four flights of stairs to our apartment. Once he was gone, my cold steadily got worse but I did not have a way to get to the dispensary. By the time he got home, I was running a high fever and nearly delirious. I cried when I saw him. He took me straight away to the dispensary where I learned I was pregnant for the second time.

I once knew a girl from our old neighborhood that had been to Germany and had a baby. This was before I had left the States. She said, "Whatever you do, don't have a baby in the Army hospital." Those words rang in my ears as we drove back from the dispensary. I was so very sick and now I had received the news that I was pregnant. It seemed things were going from bad to worse. The last six weeks had been a nightmare. Poor little Rhonda barely had a mother to care for her. She tried to help me by washing dishes herself. I can still see her standing on a stool pulled up to the sink in the kitchen washing those dishes while I was helpless to do very much more than open a few cans of soup or make a peanut butter sandwich.

It wasn't until after New Year's that we finally received our permanent quarters and fortunately we were back in Butzbach. This meant we would be close to the base and nearer to most of the necessities of military life. The military had assigned us to a huge fully furnished, second floor apartment with a balcony. When I say "huge" I mean the rooms were huge, all but the kitchen. For some reason the kitchens were small but our apartment had a large dining room and living room. The bedrooms were extremely large as well. The floors were wood and there were large area rugs in all of the rooms. The laundry rooms were all located in the basement below ground and we had certain days allotted to use the washers and dryers. I'm not sure when but at some point we were able to purchase a washer and dryer that we could install inside the apartment freeing me to wash clothes whenever I wanted. That was a blessing, thank you God. With a baby on the way, washing clothes in the apartment meant I didn't have to worry about climbing up and down stairs with all of the clothes and laundry supplies and Rhonda in tow.

Yeah, well here I was about to give birth at 97th General Hospital in Frankfurt West Germany. It was March 4th, 1973, Gary's birthday. The day had begun badly. It was a cold, damp, dreary day and I was tired and achy, my back hurt and I just plain felt like crap. I had a lot of pressure in my groin and felt as if a sack of potatoes were on my pelvis. I had never actually felt labor pains. When I had Rhonda, I had been heavily drugged and Dr. Davis had induced my labor because Gary's leave was about to end. We didn't have time to wait for things to happen naturally. I had nearly missed the whole experience because of the drugs. What I knew about labor had been erased by heavy drugs. At some point that afternoon, Gary decided I needed to see a doctor and brought me down to the dispensary in the Butzbach housing area. The doctor on duty, hearing my symptoms, told Gary I was probably in labor and he could drive me to the hospital. He added that it wasn't a rush though. Then, he took me in for a vaginal exam before releasing me to proceed to 97th Gen. In order to go to the hospital, a doctor would have to give the go ahead. We couldn't just go, we had to get permission. When he examined me I was already 3 centimeters dilated. He went back to Gary and told him to waste no time getting to Frankfurt. Off we went as fast as we could, Gary, Rhonda and me.

I had my baby that day. She came into the world screaming and crying for all she was worth. I cried a little that she wasn't a boy, then felt guilty that I had felt that way. Then, still crying I said to her, "Shhhhh little Bonnie, don't cry, Mommy loves you." Moreover, I did. I loved her terribly. She weighed 6 lbs. 15½ oz. She was a bit bigger than Rhonda had been at 6 lbs. 6 ½ oz. Rhonda hadn't cried, I guess she was as drugged as I was. The nurses wrapped Bonnie up and put her in a incubator to proceed on to be tested for all of the usual stuff they test babies for after they are born. Later, as they instructed me as to how to massage my belly after birth, Gary and Rhonda came in to see me. One of the nurses told me they were sitting outside the maternity ward looking like a couple of lost souls. She said Gary looked as white as a sheet. After a brief visit, Gary had to leave to go back home leaving me with the promise he would come back as soon as he could. He would still have to go into work as usual, Rhonda would need to go to the day care center in the housing area and I would be 45 miles away with my new baby. Back then, we stayed in the hospital for a week after having a baby.

The first couple of days were not too bad. I was in the maternity ward with about a half dozen other mothers and their new babies. We each had our own baby next to our bed in a stand that rolled around. The top part was clear plastic and looked a little like an incubator but was really the little bed for the baby. Underneath were storage drawers to keep diapers, cloths, swabs, etc. and anything we needed to help us take care of our babies and ourselves. We would get to know each other over the next few days and it was kind of fun having others with which to share this experience. When I had Rhonda, it was in Baptist Hospital in New Orleans, the same hospital where I was born. *CHAMPUS* paid for the whole thing, I had a private room and a nurse would bring Rhonda to me for feeding times. The two experiences were total opposites.

As I said, the first few days were sort of fun but one day Gary was unable to come as promised. I was unable to reach him by phone and I knew he would be going to the field again shortly after I got out of the hospital. The thought of him leaving had brought me to a state of panic I guess. I would be alone again. The last time he left for the field, I had been so very sick and this time I would be alone with Rhonda and a new baby. It was more than I could stand. As I remember it now, I became hysterical. The nurses became concerned that I wouldn't be able to care for Bonnie and told me I would have to bring her to the nursery and leave her there. That wasn't good. Only sick babies stayed in the nursery and Bonnie wasn't sick. The nurses brought in a social worker to talk to me to try and figure out what they could do for me.

All I wanted was my husband and he wouldn't be able to come. I was heartbroken that my baby had been ordered away from me. My husband wasn't there and he was going to be leaving as soon as I was out of the hospital. I would be alone for 6 weeks with a new baby and no way to get all of the necessary things people need after having a baby. I was a mess. Their advice was that I get a good night's sleep and they would see to it that Gary would be there the next day. He was bewildered at this turn of events. What had happened to his wife? I would love to tell you that all was fine now but it wasn't. Gary wasn't sent to the field but the CO wasn't happy that one of his soldiers was excused from field duty because his little wifey had cracked up after having a baby. Every crappy duty assignment to be found was given to Gary. Picking up cigarette butts, painting curbs, raking leaves, whatever the CO could come up with to make his life miserable he was going to do it. Gary never blamed me but I blamed myself for his misery. In the meantime, the social worker had assigned a mother's helper for me. She was another wife of a soldier stationed in Butzbach, she would come by during the day, we would talk, and she helped me with the girls. She even taught me how to crochet. After a while, the system deemed that I was ok to be by myself and my helper was released from her assignment. Linda was stable.

One evening, after dinner, we had a knock on the door. I opened it to find a German fellow who said he wanted to talk with me about the Bible. I asked him to wait while I asked my husband if he was interested in talking. In my mind, I just knew Gary would not be interested so was in complete shock when he said "Sure, let him in." In walked Günter Berg. He was a tall, average built, dark haired German man about Gary's age. He was pleasant and friendly and we felt comfortable with him from the start. He wanted to share his message with us and asked if he could come back again. Gary said fine and he set a time and day to return. We began a friendship that night that lasted many years. Günther was a Jehovah's Witness. When he returned, he introduced his wife Edelgard but she said to call her Edel, everyone did.

We four became fast friends. Edel was a lovely, energetic little woman. The only way I could ever describe her was that she looked very much like

Natalie Wood. Both of them were very educated and she was fluent in three languages, English, German and Russian. They were missionaries called *Special Pioneers*. The society had assigned them to the Americans stationed in Germany and they were a part of the English-speaking congregation for the Butzbach area. We all four became almost inseparable. Even though Gary couldn't accept their Bible teaching, he cared deeply about them both as friends. We had wonderful times back then and I began studying with them almost from the beginning. The Witnesses became my family. Edel and Günther were like the brother and sister I had never had. They were like the friends I had never had. Germany had now become a wonderful place to be after the nightmare I had just lived through. I cannot tell you the night and day experience of life before and after Edel and Günther. I thought I had found God. My attitude changed and Gary and I became closer as I learned to be a better wife and mother. However, we had a new thorn to bear, the thorn of the religious wife and the unbelieving husband.

The Witnesses do not believe in birthdays and all

holidays including Christmas. This was intolerable for Gary. He is a gift-giving addict. Our first Christmas, we spent every available penny on the tree and gifts for everyone including my brother. We gave him a brand new Schwinn bicycle. It was a shiny, metallic green beauty with a banana seat. Gloria had a fit that my brother got his bike and Gary's little brothers didn't get a bike too. Like I said earlier, we suffered for that bike.

The bike was just another nail in our coffin of hate we built between Gary's family and mine. By the time of our first Christmas we barely spoke. Gloria, Ann and George were my mortal enemies and did whatever they could to separate me from Gary. My poor husband was in a difficult situation. He loved his brother but only tolerated his half-sister and half-brothers. Gloria reminded him constantly that she was his mother. When describing Gloria, Gary has often quoted the lyrics of that old song the *Stones* once sang called Cloud 9. In it there is a part that says "*the mother who deserted you wants a million dollars back*". The more we tried to please her the worse she got. There are those who will say she was evil. She did do some despicable things, the first of which was blaming her own mother for all of her troubles. When I came into the family, everyone called her Gloria. Gary and George originally thought she was their sister. It wasn't until she and Bill, Ann's daddy, were leaving for Germany that it all came out. Gloria wanted Gary and George to go with her to Germany. Bill, her second husband, was being transferred there with the Air Force. It was all very dramatic. Here are the boys in the middle of a huge tug of war between mother and daughter over who is their "Mama". Gary thought his grandmother was his "Mama" and here is this woman who he believed was his sister saying, "She's not your mama, I'm your mama." Gloria had lost custody years before. She had no rights but she wanted to cause as much pain as possible because of the hate she had for her mother. Grandma had raised her own children and was older now but she gave Gary and George all the love she could.

Talking about Gary's younger brothers reminds me of something I left out. While we were still living in our temporary apartment, we received word from the Red Cross that Gary's half-brother Greg had died in a fire. There have been a couple of versions of how this happened but this was the one I heard first and the one that makes the most sense. Greg was about 21 and living in California trying to earn his living restoring furniture. He had a partner who was gay and the partner had a young son. They got into a fight and the partner with his son moved out leaving Greg alone. In a moment of anger and revenge, Greg piled up some furniture in the middle of the room, doused the pile with furniture stripper and tried to set it on fire. He became engulfed in flames and later died of the burns. Greg's death was the first tragedy to strike Gary's family but it wouldn't be the last.

There were many deaths in my family while we were in Germany. We were to be in Germany from 1972 until early 1976. In four years, we lost my grandmother, three uncles, Gary's aunt Lucille and his brother Greg. His grandmother, unable to deal with the loss of Hammond, tried to kill herself with a gun but only wounded herself in the shoulder. It was a very sad time but, if we hadn't had Günther and Edel, it would have been much worse. They helped us through some of the worst times we had in Germany.

God must have sent them even though I don't believe now that their brand of "truth" was real. Try as I might, I can't remember what I learned in all the studies I had with them. I will not say these people were evil, that would be a lie. I will say they were deluded by a false belief and I pray that they learn the truth before it is too late. I studied with Edel and Günther until it was decided I could be baptized. The baptism was in Heidelberg, Germany. That was in 1974 I believe. I found a room to stay in with a little old German woman who lived in Heidelberg who didn't speak English. She was a sweet little woman who was also a Witness. She made me feel right at home and I enjoyed my stay there. My time with the witnesses would fill a book all by itself so I won't try to put all of that in here except to say that once I left Germany, the spell was broken. I never felt the same goodness and sense of belonging I did when I was with the people who became my brothers and sisters of the Witnesses in Germany.

We left Germany in January of 1976 and America

would celebrate its 200th birthday. We were returning home with two children and would settle back in as civilians as soon as Gary finished out his enlistment. He had only a few months left. Before leaving for, where else, Aberdeen Proving Grounds, Maryland, we found an apartment in Gretna, Louisiana. I put Rhonda in school and off Gary went to finish up with Uncle Sam, assured he had a job waiting with his brother George who was the bell captain at the Marriott Hotel downtown. Everything was all set. It would only be a couple of months, what could go wrong. As they say, the best laid plans of mice and men... oft times go awry. He got out all right but the assured job did not come through. It seems management had finally decided to frown on nepotism at the Marriott. God, is that you? I certainly thought so at the time. You see, I was not happy about Gary working with George at the Marriott.

George and Mary had gotten divorced while we were in Germany. Their marriage had suffered a fatal blow years before when Mary had cheated on him. That actually happened while we were still dating. He had tasted the single life, had married again but didn't trust women at all. He had found attractive women throwing themselves at him to be very exciting. I felt that George would have liked nothing better than to get Gary away from me and into another relationship. He wanted to set Gary up more than once since our marriage and I was sure his mind hadn't changed. Gary was frustrated with my jealously. He tried to make me understand that nothing George could ever say or do would convince him to betray me or our marriage. I feared the temptation he would face and it consumed me. I prayed but I didn't trust in God that all would be well.

My first act when we arrived from Germany as I walked into my parents' house was to find a Kingdom Hall. I had gotten my life together in Germany. I went from a sniveling, trembling mass of jello unable to care for my home to someone who could cook, clean, care for her family and worship God all at the same time. I thought, "I have my life together." I didn't want to lose that. I wanted to keep the self-reliance I had found. My new faith had been a part of my growth just as the separation from my family had been. We, Gary and I both for nearly 4 years, had been unable to retreat to our families when things got tough. We had been 5,000 miles away and learned to depend on each other and not our families. My first test came quickly as I reached for the phone, like an alcoholic looking for an AA meeting, I needed the comfort of my faith. My mother reacted immediately. The Witnesses taught me to expect persecution by the world but I had not expected my own mother would see my faith as abhorrent. She, who for years had rarely gone to church, tried to make me feel as if I were doing something wrong. It was hard for me to understand. I stood my ground. I needed to be with my church and that was that. It drove us from her home and we stayed with Gloria until we found our own apartment.

The one place I didn't want to be was in the 'loving arms' of Gary's family but here we were. With all of his immediate family living on the Westbank and mine on the Eastbank in Metairie, we were light years apart. Once we found our own place, we could go back to being on our own again. I didn't know it would take years. All I knew was we had found an apartment in Gretna on the Westbank, it was near a school for Rhonda and a Kingdom Hall for me. Our things from Germany were on their way and would arrive in weeks. Gary would be home soon and all would be well. As I said, the best laid plans...

Gary didn't have a job. That was clear. We had an apartment but no money. What else could go wrong? Rhonda's school called me in for a meeting and I was told she could not catch up with the other children and would fail the first grade. Since she arrived so late in the school year and all of her first grade studies in Germany were different from those here, she would have to be kept back. No amount of reasoning on my part made any difference to the school officials. Anything else? Oh yeah, I'm pregnant. If this wasn't enough, the congregation of Witnesses were less than enthusiastic to have a new member from Germany. I wasn't exactly welcomed with open arms. Chided for having an unbelieving husband, I was now one of the poor and pitiable sisters who needed guidance by the elders. I remember one of the brothers of my old congregation in Germany telling us how wonderful the American congregations were and how friendly a southern group of the Friends would be. He was John Russell, a single American brother who was with our congregation, having stayed in Germany after getting out of the service. John spoke highly of southerners and that all would be fine. Gary was sure things would be much different and the people here would not be like those in Germany. Gary was right, John was wrong. He was dead wrong.

So many of the things I believed were wrong. First, we had all come to believe that we would never leave Germany. Edel and Günter both thought that the Kingdom would come before we left, they were wrong. John thought we would find a wonderful congregation, he was wrong. I thought that I would always have the friendship of Edel and Günter, the Isbels, Liz, Doris, Lupe, John and the Briel's. All of these and more were back in Germany, not here. Accept for Holger Briel, I have never seen any of my old friends again.

The first few months were a nightmare of uncertainty. We got on Food Stamps for a few months; Gary worked for George to earn spending money. He would go for a few hours every so often to cut grass or other odd jobs but the real motivation was to get away from me. I had become clingy and emotionally needy. Crying a great deal and worrying about what would become of us. I truly hate to tell you how bad things had become. My pregnancy was not wearing well on me this time. I actually felt good most of the time with Rhonda. With Bonnie, after the fever had passed, the worst part was that bit in the hospital. However, this time I had morning sickness daily for nearly nine months with premature labor more times than I can remember.

That summer Gary and I were further apart than we had ever been. It took an unbelievably horrific event to reunite us. On a day like many others, I was home alone with the girls, Gary was at George's cutting his grass I believe when the phone rang. It was my mother. I know it was early afternoon because mother said she had just been watching the Channel 4 News noon report. She asked me where was Gary's brother, Glenn? Had he left town? I said no, I didn't think so, why? She told me she had heard that a Glenn Davis from New Orleans was shot and killed in Spokane, Washington. "Mother, how many

Glenn Davis's do you think there are in the world? That is a very common name. I'm sure there are many Glenn Davis's in New Orleans. The chances of that being Glenn is ridiculous." Even so, she was determined that I call George and ask him if Glenn had gone to Spokane. I hesitated for a few minutes trying to work up the nerve to dial the phone. It was the very last thing I wanted to do. Gary and I were barely speaking. I had called him many times at George's over the last few months and he was sick of my intrusions. I had determined not to call and anger him any further. Nevertheless, here was my own mother knowing how things were, asking me to do the one thing that was sure to make things worse. Just the sound of my voice on the phone that day made George sigh with annoyance. His patience with me at an end, he asked "What?" when I said his name. "George?" "What?" he asked. "Look, I'm not trying to bother you or anything but is Glenn in town? Or, did he leave?" I tried to explain. "Why?", he replied. "Well, my mother just called and said she heard on the news that a Glenn Davis of New Orleans had been shot and killed in Spokane Washington. I told her there are lots of Glenn Davis's but she insisted that I call and ask you." To this day, I can hear his voice as he said, "You're shittin me?" There was a long pause, then he finally said, "Call the TV station and see if they have any more information." I did just that and he galvanized the effort to see if this was our Glenn.

Gloria was traveling in Mexico with her latest husband Efrain. He would ultimately be her last husband. She needed to be located in order for her to learn her youngest son was dead. George had indeed found out that Glenn's girlfriend, Denise, had murdered him during an argument while they were visiting her family in Spokane. He was dead. The officials were trying to find his family and had put out a wire report, which our local CBS news station aired that day. My mother had been the only one to hear the report. The rest you know.

First Greg, now Glenn, and each had died at the same age, 21, under horrible circumstances. Looking back at all of this in the clarity of the passage of time, it helps me to understand so much. I love it when I hear people say "Why did God let this happen?" or "Why didn't God stop that from happening?" Whatever the trouble or the horrible thing we have in our own lives, or of someone else's life, it seems humans first blame God. How ironic. It reminds me of Adam. Ever since Adam, people have looked for someone else to blame for their troubles. In Genesis 3:12, after God finds Adam and Eve hiding from him and asked him if they had eaten from the tree, what did Adam say? He says, "Yeah but it's your fault, that woman you gave me, she made me do it." Is it any wonder he kicked them to the curb? Since then, man has been blaming God for everything. Give me a break, the only blameless one *is* God. Even sickness and death, that was Adam's choice not God's fault. He ate what wasn't his to eat. If he had just said, "God, I ate it and I'm sorry. Please forgive me, it won't happen again." We would all still be living in paradise. However, he didn't and look where we are now, a life of toll and strife, sickness and death all because Adam couldn't say "I'm sorry." Still, we want to blame God first. Even now, when God has given us a way out, we still don't want to take it. God sent Jesus to earth to give us a way out. All we need to do is take it. Just accept the gift. For us to say truly, *"Dearest God, I'm sorry for all that I have done and I accept your gift of Jesus."* just that much is too hard for us to do. Rather, it is easier for us to deny God exists, it is easier for us to hate Him for our own human imperfection, our own sickness, our own death and it is easier for us to hurt our fellow man and turn around and say, "It is God's fault all of this is happening." No, no, no, *we* have done this and that's why it is happening. Greg and Glenn didn't have to die the way they did. We all had a hand in their deaths but mostly their own poor choices were to blame, not God.

The family gathered from all over. Bill, Glenn's dad, was in a nursing home. Ann was living in Colorado. After dating for a number of years, she and Tommy had married, he decided to join the Air Force and they now had three children. Michelle was their oldest daughter. Tommy, their son, was in the middle and Angelia was the youngest. By this time, Grandma was in a nursing home and not interested in very much. Ever since her Hammond had passed away, she was just waiting to die. With the funeral set, we all gathered at Laughlin's Funeral Home on Magazine Street that summer of 1976. The uncles and aunts, cousins, nieces and nephews, brothers and sisters, mothers and fathers and Glenn's little son Glenn Ray with his mother Anna, Glenn's ex-wife, assembled to say good-bye. The scene was so very sad.

The afternoon of the wake began as these things usually do with everyone speaking in hushed tones, and tears shed here and there, as mourners filled the viewing area. As the afternoon wore on, most of the family decided to go outside for air and the occasion to smoke and visit with each other away from the somber casket setting at the back of the main viewing room. New Orleans in late summer is stifling and in my condition, I preferred staying inside where it was cool. This was the very room where Daddy-Oh was set so many years before. I can only think it was better that Grandma hadn't come to see her grandson in this room. I remember sitting in the window box seat at the front of the room and seeing the casket at the far end of this long, main viewing room. I wasn't alone. Along with my two little girls, Gloria and I had decided to remain behind.

We sat in silence for a time. The girls were antsy and didn't want to be here but I hung on so as not to be alone with Gloria. She got up and proceeded to walk the long way to the casket. I could hear her talking in a soft, quiet voice to her son in his coffin. It wasn't clear what she was saying at first but then she bent over the casket and began attempting to sit him up saying, "Come on Glenn, let's get up and go home." Wait, what did she say? Oh my God, this was NOT good. I got up and ran as quickly as I could in my condition to stop her. She seemed determined to get him out. I then turned to Rhonda and told her to go as fast as possible to find her daddy and tell him to come now. I needed him. Before I knew it, others were there and were able to stop her before she pulled Glenn out. The rest of the day was a blur. The following morning Gloria, on the way to the cemetery, decided to add insult to injury by begging me for my unborn baby. She insisted I was going to have another girl that I didn't want. She wanted a baby to replace the one she had lost and she would be a better parent than we were. She wanted my baby. She of all the people in the world was demanding my baby. Gary quickly told her to shut up. He would give her the respect of not telling her off as she deserved but he forcefully demanded that she stop, she could not have our baby. The only one of her five children she actually had raised was Ann. She'd had five opportunities. Four boys and one girl, but all she had ever wanted was girls. The first two boys she dumped on her mother. The other two she put in foster homes or religious halfway houses and state run psychiatric institutions for most of their lives. Was it any wonder that they had both met tragic ends? Once the funeral was over, our duty done, Gary and I escaped to our apartment and found ourselves reunited with a new, closer bond between us. Gone was the distance we had been experiencing since his discharge from the Army and all of the hard feelings we had built up seemed small and unimportant now.

Now that we were back to being a family again Gary found a GI bill program that paid him to go to welding school with the promise of a job when the course was over. The course was more of a refresher for him than anything new. After completing the course, he got a part time job right away as a contract welder. We were finally able to feel a tiny bit better financially. This wasn't full time work but it would do until a permanent position could become available. Some months later, Gary found his first job with something called a fishing tool company in Harvey. He had no idea this would be what he would do for the rest of his career.

I spent my time dreaming of a home of our own and combing the newspapers for ads of homes for sale. One day, there in a tiny little square, was an ad for new homes. I wish I had saved that newspaper ad. All I can remember was thinking we could do this. I called the number and went to where the man told me I could see him about the homes. It was located in Marrero, not far from where we were living in Gretna and in Harvey where Gary worked.

It took quite a bit of doing, but we got our new house. The first time I went out there, all of the houses were still bare bones. Literally, they were bare bones. The man I had spoken to on the phone took me to a construction area at the back of the subdivision. This was where the new houses were under construction. I had no idea what to expect, but I didn't expect that the homes would have no walls or roofs. They were nothing more than a slab with studs. There weren't many of them at that time. Home construction had not begun on most of the new streets. The street he took me to was a block long and lined with new homes in various stages of construction from just the slab to a slab with studs. I looked at each one, measuring the "walls", looking for one that would work. I needed one wall to be long, especially long. While we were in Germany, we had purchased a few things that were uniquely German. One of them was called a "shrunk". A German shrunk is a piece of wooden furniture that takes up an entire wall. Being so large, it came in pieces. Whenever we moved, we had to take it apart and re-assemble it. Our shrunk was a combination of many things that included a bookshelf, cabinets, huge deep storage drawers, a curio cabinet and even had a small bar for mixing drinks. Ours wasn't real wood, only pressed particleboard, but it was a beauty when assembled. I had to find a living room wall that would accommodate that shrunk. When I did, that was the house for us. The only floor plan that had a wall long enough had 3 bedrooms and 2 baths, it would be a brick home the man said and would have a garage. The price, only $26,800. Even in 1976, that was a great deal. I could not explain how I had found this except to say God was finally smiling on us. We had been through so much since our marriage but finally we could have a home to put all of us in. That's what I thought but Gary didn't really expect much to come of this dream of mine. All he would say was, "Go ahead and try, if you want, but don't get your hopes up." He couldn't see how we would be able to buy a home since we had no money saved and barely any furniture. We had been living on the edge since he got out of the Army. Gary had only had his new job a couple of months and here I was talking about us buying a house. Sometimes we just have to have faith. We were able to scrape together the $150 deposit and used Gary's benefits to submit an application for a VA loan. We had very little furniture of our own. The few things we had when we moved into our apartment, along with donated furniture from our families and the gift of a stove and refrigerator my parents had promised to give us, we would have just enough to set up housekeeping at the new house. These were the dreams I had to hold onto. As the weeks passed, I would drive out to the construction site watching my house go up bit by bit. I knew every inch of it. I walked every foot of the grounds, measured every wall, saw the pipes for the bathtubs and sinks, the wires for the wall sockets, everything. This was *my* house. The closer it came to completion, the more convinced I became that this was our new home. All the while, I was getting closer and closer to having my baby and we were getting closer and closer to our new home. About two months out, I got word that we were denied the loan by the VA. Their reason was Gary hadn't been working long enough at his current job and we had no money in the bank. This was a crushing blow. I don't remember calling on Jehovah but I must have prayed long and hard that God show me the way. What was I going to do? How could I get around this? I thought what if I went to Gary's boss. Would he consider writing a letter stating that Gary was an excellent worker with a secure future with the company? Chester Lewis was a kind man who liked Gary very much. He really did think Gary was a hard worker who had a future with the company. Chester saw that Gary worked long hours and never missed work. He knew we were a young couple with two children and one on the way. Yes, he said he would help. He wrote a wonderful letter for me to send to the VA people. With that secured, I went to my dad for a favor. My idea was to ask him if he would briefly loan me the $1000 he had promised for the purchase of the new stove and refrigerator. I would then put it in the bank long enough for it to post to our account. Once it was on paper, I could send this to the VA and then give the money right back to daddy. It made perfect sense and there was absolutely no risk for anyone.

On the day I decided to put my idea to my dad, I got in the old car we brought back from Germany and drove across the Mississippi river to Magazine Street to daddy's shoe shop. When I walked in, he was, as usual, busy behind his counter working on a pair of shoes. The little shop always smelled heavily of leather cement, new leather and shoe polish. His machines were whirring loudly as he buffed and sanded at the soles of his customer's shoes preparing to attach a new half-sole and heel. As I walked up the steps and into the shop, I must have looked like the beached whale I felt like but, I didn't care. It seemed as though I couldn't help getting bigger each time I had a baby. This time I topped 175 lbs. I came through the door and up to the counter as I had done a million times in my life. Daddy turned and said "wuss-up?" in his usual manner. I can see the stern look and I know I am in for a bit of a tussle over this but, my logic is sound and he will have no risk whatever. I know my daddy, he was a cheap *dago*, as stingy as they come. He would rather work all day making a new handle for his broom than spend the money to buy a new one. Never mind that in the time he took to make it he would have made enough money to buy 10 brooms or more. Asking him for money was tantamount to stealing. His response was "Get the hell outa here with your shit, girl. I ain't got no time for your shit." "But daddy" I cried. "Naw, naw, naw, I don't wanna hear it, get outa here. Go home". As I left the city, those words hung over me all the way back across the river. I cried bitterly all the way home. Now what was I going to do, he was my only way to show the VA I had money in the bank. I had to think. There was no way I had come this far and not get my house. We would soon have the third baby and that apartment was a hellhole. I could not stand living there any longer. What would I do? Think Linda, you need to show the VA there is money in the bank. That $1000 would have been the perfect solution. Barring that, how could I show money in our account? Then it hit me, Gary's checks were the largest they had ever been. However, by the time they cleared I would have already written checks to pay our bills and nearly all of the money would be gone within a day or two. I thought 'what if I deposited his check, took the deposit slip to a bank officer, had him certify that the money was there and write a brief statement to that affect then send that to the VA'? Would that do the trick? Would that satisfy the government's loan officer? I am here to tell you that is exactly what happened. I had done it and without my dad. We had our last daughter on January 21, 1977 and moved into our new home at the end of February 1977. Now all we had to do was keep it.

Sandra was born that January after having so many false starts. Perhaps it was the stress of Gary being out of work, the death of Glenn or all the ups and downs to do with getting the house but I had a number of episodes of false labor. I was just glad that finally it was all over. She was a beautiful little strawberry blond with blue-gray eyes. Rhonda was born with a full head of blond hair, almost white really. Bonnie had brown hair and brown eyes, now Sandra was here and had a tiny hint of pink to her blond hair, each of them beautiful but different. I had my hands full for sure as both of the two oldest were hyperactive and now I had this little one and we would be moving into our new home in a few weeks. It was a great deal to have to handle all at once.

We moved in by the hardest. No thanks to the Gretna congregation of witnesses I belonged to. In Germany, we were a family, here, not so much. This fact only added to my growing disappointment and to the fear that something just wasn't right. I had begun to doubt my faith. As the days, weeks and months went by that year, my prayers began to be begging sessions. I pleaded with God to show me what I was doing wrong. "Please God, help me. I need you God. Please show me what I am doing wrong." I remember being in the shower with the hot water streaming down my face mixing with my tears, the sound of the shower covering up my sobs and my pleas for help. I found it harder and harder to talk to anyone, especially the brothers and sisters of my new congregation. When I moved from Gretna to Marrero, I had to change congregations. Those were the rules. I was in trouble, my faith was slipping away and no matter how hard I tried, I couldn't get a grip on things. The people in my new congregation were tired of my complaints so I stopped. I just stopped. No more, I had had enough.

6

The Atheist

Atheism: lack of belief in God or active disbelief in God ... you see that last part, that's it. I had come full circle. I had decided if God had not heard me that he must not be there. As far as I was concerned, that was the only answer. After all, what was I asking for? I wasn't asking for wealth, power or position. I was asking for help, the peace of God during a time of great turmoil in my life. Isn't this one of the main things God was supposed to have promised us? So, he must not exist and I have been wasting my time.

Once I had made up my mind, I proceeded to let everyone know I was through with religion. My family was horrified. They blamed Gary. He made me do it. My mother, who hated my choice of religions, blamed him. She couldn't believe I had made such a decision on my own. The Witnesses blamed him. Did I know what I was doing? I was told often enough over the years what happens to a disfellowshiped witness. Their lives became worse than a non-believers. Their lives are living hell on earth. It wasn't uncommon to see one in the gutter. Even my next-door neighbor blamed Gary thinking I did it to please him. No, I hadn't. I did it because I had lost my faith. I felt alone, empty.

I know all about alone. I felt alone as a young girl, thinking I would never find my one true love to share my life with. I felt alone in Germany. The first time Gary went to the field, I remember staring out of the windows into the courtyard of the housing area and thinking how many others were so close but still I felt so alone. Inside myself, I felt alone. It's like walking in a forest and the only sound you hear is the sound of your own breathing or the snap of the twig under your foot. You know you are alone. If you cried out, no one would hear you, that kind of alone.

Inside myself, I had always been alone and it was time to grow up and face it.

I began by picking up a cigarette. When I began my studies with Edel and Günther, I was a smoker. Quitting was a requirement if I wanted to become a Witness. I always loved smoking but gave it up for my new faith. Now, there was no reason not to start again. Besides, I had gained a ton of weight since quitting. I had picked up most of it while pregnant with Sandra. Smoking again, I reasoned, would help me loose the weight I was now carrying. I hated being fat so why not smoke. This was actually putting me on the fast track to being removed from my faith. Smoking was a disfellowshiping offense. Being disfellowshiped is the Witness's form of excommunication. It did not take long, and when it was over, I would become one of the shunned. That was fine with me. Those in the congregation who were insecure in their faith would actually run from me when they saw me coming. This silly game actually made me laugh on more than one occasion.

I now went about my business with a resolve to do as others do, raise my girls, take care of my business, stay out of other people's business and be a good wife to my husband. Gary was always happy about that part of the religion. He loved having an obedient wife but hated the religious part. This was great in his mind since I did not intend to become a loose woman just because I no longer believed in God. He was also relieved since he had always worried about the blood issue. Witnesses did not, do not, believe in blood transfusions. Other tenets of the religion are not serving in the military and not celebrating holidays and birthdays among other things. It's the whole separate yourself from the world thing. Anyway, I wasn't planning a full-scale plunge into decadence. I wanted to be a good person but didn't need a crutch to do it, or so I thought.

I did pretty well at first. I had managed to be an acceptable housekeeper but, not as good as I was in Germany. As a mother, I did not feel I was up to the task. I had three hyperactive girls. It was like having three little white tornados tearing through my life at once. It strained the nerves to have these little girls in constant motion every waking moment. I was relieved as they began to all be in school at the same time. I thought that finally I would have some quiet time to myself. It wasn't that they were bad really, just active. They couldn't seem to be still for 2 minutes.

Rhonda was the first to slow down. Up until now, she had been skinny. However, at around ten she slowed to a crawl and began to put on weight. Gary's genes and my mother's genes finally caught up with her. Yes, my gorgeous hunky husband had a weight problem. Any time we were together, he would eat whatever and whenever which caused him to gain an enormous amount of weight. It had become more of a problem while we were in the Army. Whenever we were together, he would put on the pounds. When he was away from me though, he just had no appetite. To make matters worse, I am a great cook, no joke. My mother on the other hand had been born heavy. She battled a weight problem until the day she died. She had discovered she had diabetes in the 1960's after we were in an automobile accident coming home from a trip to see Mama. Mother had been hurt the worst and was admitted to the hospital. During the blood work and urinalysis, the doctors discovered she had Type 2 diabetes. This news only added to her many other health problems. None of us had health insurance back then. In fact, I didn't know about health insurance until the military insurance I received by being married to Gary. What is considered a necessity today, no dare I say a RIGHT by some, back then was a luxury. I do have an example of this but it isn't worth going into now.

Rhonda became a slug, would that the other two would as well, maybe I would get some peace. Not really, I wouldn't wish her weight problems on all of my girls but only that they slow down as she had. Gary was very heavy, now Rhonda was too and I was still chunky, so the smoking hadn't worked as I had hoped. All in all life just wasn't very peaceful for any of us from 1977 to 1986.

Gary worked hard to support his family. His work for fishing tool companies was dependent on the oil industry. Perhaps I should explain what fishing tools are. Fishing is a term used to describe what takes place when a foreign object becomes lodged in an oil well obstructing the hole so that no oil can be brought out. This object is called a "fish" hence the term "fishing". The company that is drilling the well hires a fishing tool company to solve the problem. The fishing tool company sends out an operator who has been trained to assess the situation. He must determine a way to remove the "fish". Once this happens, someone must construct the "tool" that will best suite this particular problem. My husband had the job to "dress" the "tool" that "cuts" up the "fish" that is stuck in the "hole". To "dress" a "tool" means to apply tungsten carbide to the areas of the "tool" that will cut up the "fish" and clear the hole. There, that was simple, right? Gary was a carbide welder for fishing tool companies. He was the best carbide man on the canal and he hated his job. I know hate is a strong word but if there were a better word for it, I would have used that one. He did it because he was a good man who loved his family and would do whatever it took to provide for them. Being a carbide welder paid well. This job was a 24/7, 52 weeks a year job. Until the early 2000's, we didn't take vacations. Back then, a phone call or his beeper usually interrupted holidays for him. I cannot tell you how many times we would just be sitting down to Thanksgiving or Christmas' dinner and the phone would ring and he would be called to go out on a hot job. He worked a regular 6 day week but, after hours, he would still be on call. During peak times, "hot" jobs would mean he would have to stay and work through the night and into days on end until the job was finished. Many times, he would leave work only to have me meet him at his truck when he got home to tell him work had called and he had to turn around and go back. The work was back breaking and hot. Almost daily, he would get burned by sparks of hot metal or get flecks of metal in his eyes as well as flash burns. He breathed in fumes that would wreck another man's lungs and get fume sickness which caused him to have hours of bone breaking chills. There's more but, you get the general idea. My job was to stay home, cook and clean, take care of the children, pay the bills and decide how best to spend whatever we had left. After a time, I couldn't do my job. I was a failure. What was worse, I added my failure to his plight.

There's nothing like having a crazy wife. My downfall began, I believe, in 1978. We had our first flood. May 3rd 1978 our area received what was a record-breaking amount of rainfall in a 24-hour period. News reports called it a 100-year event. It left our home with nearly 3 feet of water in it. We actually flooded 3 times, '78, '80 and '82. After the flood in '78, I had my first surgery. This one was for gallstones. It is remarkable to me how differently my surgery was from the way the surgery is done today. My body was cut open and I was in the hospital for weeks. Just a few weeks ago, my next-door neighbor had surgery for gallstones. She went in early one morning, the doctors made a few tiny incisions, removed the stones, etc. and she was home that afternoon. How things have changed.

The years between 1978 and 1986 were the darkest of my life. As I said, it began with the first flood, then my surgery. In 1980 came flood number two. Our finances were always rocky back then but in 1981, we needed more money so I began working at various Time Savers in this area. I had no marketable skills then. I hadn't learned to type yet and, other than my intelligence, had nothing to recommend me. My only choice was an entry-level cashier position. I worked the night shifts at three different locations before finally leaving the company. That year in January, George, arrested for scalping Sugar Bowl tickets, lost his job. This set in motion a series of events that led to drugs, alcohol and finally a bullet. In September 1981, one morning after work, the phone rang. I was taking a long hot bath after putting in a hard night. It was my habit to have the phone by the tub when alone in case I needed help. It was Pete, a friend of George's at the Marriott, calling to tell us George was dead. The police had called the Marriott, I believe, because of some contact information found on him when they discovered his body. As I sat there stunned, all I could think was to call Gary. I called and got him brought to the phone and told him to come home right away. He insisted I tell him why. It was my hope that I could persuade him to come without telling him the reason, but it didn't work. In the end, he refused to come unless I said why. I told him his brother was dead. This wasn't Greg or Glenn this was George. He grew up with this brother. The other two were raised separately from them. Somehow, he made it home. I cannot tell you the torment he had just been through with George and the drug overdoses and narrow escapes with death. Since he lost his job, George had become a different person. He had lost his identity, his self-worth was zero. However, this was finally the worst. He had ended his own life in his car with his gun and Gary had lost his last brother.

The funeral set, we went to the nursing home to tell Grandma. The home was in Slidell and in all the years she had been there, no matter how hard we tried, we could not get her to visit our new home. However, this visit was different. We had come to tell her George was gone. Poor Grandma, she had raised them the best she could, but now she had to hear the worst news possible. All she could do was cry. In January 1982, she too would pass. She finally had her wish and she was with Hammond now.

In the spring of 1982, we suffered our last flood and my next surgery. This time it was for kidney stones. I would rather have 10 dry sockets and a dozen babies sideways than have kidney stones. After the events of the past few years, I found myself in an even deeper depression than ever before. That is to say, it didn't come upon me all at once, it came on gradually until at some point I was so very depressed that I could see no way out. My mental state was such that I felt buried alive in a deep dark pit. The sides of my pit were damp, dark and close. I could actually visualize my pit, that is how very real it was. Try as I might, I could not see any daylight above. Buried alive, and with no way out, I spent my days in bed unable to function. All day long, when most people were doing what functioning members of society normally do, I lay huddled in a ball with a lump in my throat the size of a baseball that made me feel as though I were choking. The housework undone, the laundry undone, the shopping undone, I was barely able to pay the bills, that is to say, write the checks and mail them. Cooking was almost nonexistent. I would throw together what passed for a meal only on occasion, other times I called for a scrounge day. That was my way of saying scrounge for your selves, I am not able to cook. It was not a pretty sight. I was ruining my husband's life and my children's lives. There came the night that I finally decided my life wasn't worth living and I overdosed on pills. Gary had gotten a call to go to work. This was a hotshot call, which meant he would pick up a tool order at the shop and bring it to a meet in Venice. From there it would go to the rig. I knew these runs well and knew he would be gone for hours. He had asked me to go but I had refused. The girls wanted to go however, that left me alone. I took this opportunity to attempt to end my life. Everyone would be better off without me was the reason I gave for my decision.

I planned everything down to how I would take the pills. Shortly after Gary and the girls left, I opened the drawer to my nightstand next to my bed and pulled out all of my pills. I cannot tell you what I took but it was definitely enough to kill me. I had heard that taking too many pills at one time would cause me to throw up before the pills could get into my system. I decided to take a few pills at a time, waiting a short time for them to go down and then take more until I had taken all of the pills. It worked. I didn't throw up any of them. By the time Gary and the girls got home, I was out. I had left a suicide note before I passed out but it was under the sheets. The next morning my mother showed up to help me clean my house. After a while had gone by, Rhonda tried to wake me and discovered the note.

I was rushed to West Jeff Hospital. My stomach was pumped and I was admitted to the psych ward for observation and evaluation. I still wasn't thinking clearly but, after being chastised by Gary for such a selfish stunt, I did sort of pull out of the self-pity I was wallowing in. I listened to him and his advice on how to get myself out of the fix I found myself in. If I didn't get released, I would be committed and go to a psychiatric hospital in Mandeville. That thought was even worse than what I was currently dealing with so I listened.

I was released from the hospital only to be put on heavy antidepressants. All I wanted was to feel normal again. I felt like a zombie on all of these drugs. I went to the ordered group therapy sessions, took my pills and sat there listening about how it was my husband's fault, my parents fault or my kids fault but, it wasn't ever my fault. I knew I wasn't normal but I also knew deep down inside that it wasn't anyone else's fault either. What I would not understand until a few weeks later was that something was physically wrong with my body. My menstrual cycles were way off and may have been for some time but I had been too depressed to notice. Somehow, the thought came into my mind that something was amiss which caused me to have the presence of mind to make an appointment to see Dr. Davis. I hadn't paid attention as my body was telling me something was wrong but I had missed it. *Is that you God?* My periods were too close together. Dr. Davis decided it would be best to put me on birth control pills to regulate my periods. I continued to take my antidepressants for another year. I took the birth control faithfully each day. Unfortunately, the day came that my periods broke through even the pills. By this time, Dr. Davis had stopped practicing. He had had a stroke shortly after my last visit. I had trusted him for as long as I had been alive. His was the first face I saw. He delivered me into this world. He was the only doctor who had ever understood me. I had to find another doctor but I would never again find another Dr. Davis.

A friend referred a doctor near my home, he diagnosed that I needed a hysterectomy. He told me my uterus was twice it's normal size and prolapsed.

Surgery was the only treatment. This was not something I wanted, in fact, fear gripped every fiber of my being. Most of my life I had watched my mother go through a kind of perpetual menopause. Her hot flashes, mood swings and crying spells were indelibly etched in my mind. I had just come through, though badly for sure, the worst period of my life only to hear that I needed a hysterectomy. Would the same experience I witnessed my mother go through be mine as well? With tears streaming down my face and choking my voice, I expressed my fears to this new doctor. In his best bedside manner he explained that he didn't have any reason to believe he would need to remove my ovaries, just my uterus. Of course, he wouldn't know for sure until he performed the surgery but, there was hope. I clung to that hope as I went under the anesthesia. When I came to, I learned that indeed my doctor needed to remove one ovary. He said it too was twice it's normal size as well as having hair and teeth in it. That description created visions in my mind that were hard to erase. After the surgery, I promptly went into menopause. I was worse than ever. Not only was I deeply depressed and on antidepressants but now, I was having hot flashes, crying jags and mood swings. When I went in for my first post-surgery checkup, Dr. Beebe told me what I needed was hormones. I would feel better and look better but I would need to give it some time. It might take a few weeks to get completely in my system. This promise was nothing new. 'Just take this new medication and everything will be much better'. 'This newer drug is better than the one you're taking'. I had been on antidepressants for years with many promises of things getting better but never did. This new pill would be no different. All of these thoughts passed through my mind as I walked out of my doctor's office that day. In spite of my misgivings, I took the prescription slip to the drug store, had it filled and came home that day feeling as hopeless as ever. My pit was just as dark and deep. I was hopelessly doomed. As I took the first hormone pill that afternoon, I knew this little pill would never work.

What is this? The lump in my throat is smaller. "My lump, it isn't choking me like yesterday," I thought as I opened my eyes the next morning. "Can this be real? Wait, don't be a fool, you must be imagining this. Nevertheless, I do feel better, just a little bit better." I took another pill. The next day the lump was even smaller. By the end of the week, not only was the lump gone but also I was almost happy. That was most definitely different. I can now tell you, I had to wait months before I would tell anyone for fear that it wouldn't last. I had disappointed so many in my family over the years and just couldn't do that to them again. I wouldn't allow myself to reveal this recent development until I was certain it was real. As each day got better and better, it became apparent this was absolutely real, I had finally arrived. I was normal again. I could do all of the things other women did. I cooked, I cleaned, I took care of the bills. I was able to handle the day to day of being a wife and mother and I did it with joy and happiness. People could tell I had changed. No deep, dark pits, no more lumps and no more antidepressants. All I had needed from the beginning was hormones. I have never looked back. Thank you, God.

Soon I was looking for more to do. By 1989, I decided to go back to school and get some training. We needed another income but there were no jobs available for someone without skills. I enrolled in a vocational technical school for secretarial studies. I applied myself energetically and enthusiastically to my courses. I took typing, shorthand, computer science, word-processing and business math, as well as a number of other lesser courses like filing. School wasn't something I had enjoyed as a child but now I studied hard and graduated with a 4.0 average. Gary was as supportive as possible and proud of my accomplishments. Before graduation, I had to decide what I wanted to do with my new skills, some area I felt would suite me. I had an opportunity to go on a field trip to a downtown brokerage firm and liked what I saw. I found this area of the business world exciting and it opened up a new world to me. I believed I would like working in this field and so, just before graduation, I found a job with a brokerage firm downtown.

7

Betrayal and Forgiveness

In January of 1990, I found myself as the receptionist of a local office of a brokerage firm in the city. It was the start of a new chapter in my life. I wanted to work my way beyond the front desk and so lobbied the head of the municipal bond department for a position as a trading assistant. Not long after, I got a position with him in the secondary bond market. Once there, I pushed myself to improve my knowledge in this new world I had entered. I found some of those I worked with eager to help. Others resented my audacity. Who was this 40-year-old woman coming into their territory thinking she could do the work they had been doing for years. Undaunted, I applied myself with all of the determination I could muster. I took on more and more responsibility and learned quickly the tasks I needed to. Gary supported all of my efforts and went out of his way to bring me to work each day. In order to get my work done, I invested in a home computer. I learned every software program used in the office. I began studying for the Series 7 broker's license as well as taking on all of the tasks assigned to me vigorously. I guess I figured I had to make up for all the time I had lost.

Gary tried to warn me that the corporate world was dangerous but I am sad to say I didn't listen to him. I became obsessed with my job. I lost weight, worked longer and longer hours, lost sleep by studying long into the night for the broker's test. In the end, I lost all reason as to who I was and what I wanted from this job. Along the way, I also found myself obsessed with one particular person as well. He saw a weakness in me and took advantage of my delusion. I will not say I was not to blame, I was. I had lost sight of where I came from and where I was going. I lost sight of reality and nearly lost my marriage and my whole world.

Gary had given me his all. As I was going down the drain, he sensed that something wasn't right. He did everything he could think of to help but, still, I was spiraling out of control. I could hide my obsession but not the stress I was under and he could see it. In true Gary fashion, he bent over backwards for me and in the end, when I finally confessed everything, he helped me to find my way back to reality. He showed me the game that was being played against me. I had been so very naïve. Nothing in my life's experience could have prepared me for the world of financial corporations or the "dog-eat-dog" office politics of big business. I was a babe in the woods that was full of hungry wolves.

I was fortunate that I didn't cross the final line. In the end, I had lost the respect of my family, deeply hurt my husband and left the job that had nearly destroyed me. Once gone, I set about repairing all the damage I had done, started sleeping more, gained back some of the drastic weight loss, tried to make it at another firm but, in the end, we were financially bankrupt because of the mistakes I had made.

We found ourselves so deeply in debt that bankruptcy was our only solution. After a series of office jobs and even a stint at selling cars, I finally settled down with a local funeral home as the office manager. With my back firmly turned against God, I trudged along trying to mend our ruined financial life and our shattered marriage. Gary and I were still together but I had nearly destroyed his belief in my love for him. It would be my mission to do everything in my power to make it up to him. In a few short months, I had destroyed a trust built up for over 25 years. It would take time and it wouldn't be easy. The only thing we had left were each other and our love.

The funeral home was my last job. I never worked for anyone else again and this is how it happened. It is 1996, after bouncing from job to job since leaving the financial world, I answered an ad to manage the office of a funeral home in the city. This funeral home occupied a beautiful old building and had been a funeral home for over 120 years. Something about the old mansion suited me, I found it pleasant and peaceful. Even though the staff insisted the building was haunted, I enjoyed being there even when no one else was. I think I enjoyed it best when I was alone. After what I had put myself through, this was so very peaceful and quiet. I guess you could say I was looking to get as far away as possible from where I had been that I literally went to the grave. However, like everything in life, nothing is as it appears. Shortly before I had been hired, the company had been gobbled up by a huge funeral corporation and was about to go through some drastic changes. The corporation needed to cut expenses and one way was to cut hours and personnel. Not my job, of course, but my hours were cut. They did cut some staff, which resulted in more work for me, but less time to do my regular work plus the additional tasks. I again found myself coming in earlier and earlier in order to complete all of the work that was now my responsibility. Of course, I would be off the clock doing this work. It was my choice. You see, I have this thing about doing a good job. It goes back to Daddy calling me stupid and my never finishing what I start. It was a matter of being good enough. If I couldn't do the job exactly as the bosses wanted me to, I was a failure, right? Here I sat in a new job but things were beginning to look all too familiar. The old pressures to be on top of everything and striving to be all things at all times was back. This was exactly what I did not want. Just as I had gotten to my breaking point, on the 28th of October, my mother passed away. Just when I thought I could take this stress no longer, I had the perfect job to do the final act for the mother who had given me life. I would be seeing her out of this world. I set about doing the typing and arraigning that I had learned to do for others. I wrote the details of her life, typed up the death certificate, submitted the obituary to the paper and made the arraignments for the clothing and flowers and, well, everything. Was it by design, I don't know. I just know that one night I found myself working with the mortician to make sure that Mother looked just as she should. The night before my mother's funeral, I helped with her makeup, hair and even tweezed her mole as I had seen her do all of my life. She hated the little hairs that grew in the mole on her face. Mother wasn't a pretty woman, she had been a big baby and a chubby little girl with freckles and red haired. During her life, she would go up and down in weight but would never succeed in losing the weight. However, she was a wonderful cook. Our entire extended family enjoyed meals prepared by my mother. She would create such wonderful meals with deep love and affection. Her cooking skills were legend. Everyone had their favorites and I had learned most of her secrets. She was also skilled in sewing, which I hadn't learned but Shirley, my sister, had. Mother made many of our clothes when we were young. We had our differences over the years and it would be nice to say that we parted as friends but I cannot. I am so very sorry to say that she had no idea who I was the last time I saw her alive. She died alone and in a nursing home not knowing anyone. Her diabetic condition had robbed her of her health, her eyes, her leg and her mind. I think she just gave up in the end. She just didn't want to live anymore. She didn't try anymore. Her family laid Mother to rest on Thursday, October 31, 1996. She was survived by her husband of 48 years, her three children and five grandchildren. I have yet to cry.

The next morning, after her funeral, as I sat at my desk I knew, in my heart, I could not do this anymore. The old funeral home was silent. No one else had arrived yet. I sat there thinking over the last 3 days, a wave of resignation came crashing down on me. I'd had enough of trying to succeed in the working world. Knowing how badly I felt, Gary and I had talked about this and he had told me we would be able to make ends meet without my paycheck. He would get more hours, and with the bankruptcy, there would be fewer bills. I know it was wrong, even cowardly, but I took a blank sheet of paper from the copy machine, wrote a note that said I was leaving, taped it to my desk and walked out. I never looked back.

8

The Business Woman

I drove myself home that Friday morning and, with each mile, the stress dissolved. By the time I got home, I was drained and numb. I had resolved never again to get myself into anything remotely resembling a job. No sir, working was not for me. I couldn't handle the stress of a job. I still have to figure out what to do with myself but, whatever it might be, it would not include a boss.

I need to go back a bit here and mention that my mother and father had moved a number of years before. Back in the time after my rescue from the pit but before going back to school, Mother had a stroke.

Before her stoke, we were best friends. She and I talked every day and got along very well. Other than Gary, I was closer to her than to anyone else in my life. Teenage girls do not make friends with their mother's so my daughters and I were not friends back then. Mother was it for me. Therefore, this particular day, late afternoon really, my nasty little brother called to say that mother was acting funny. Her speech was slurred and her face looked strangely pulled on one side. My first thought was she'd had a stroke and said so. He scoffed and made some sort of remark like "How do you know, you're not a doctor." You don't need to be a doctor to figure that out. Long story short, after a long stay in the hospital recovering from her stroke, Mother was adamant that she and Daddy needed to move. My brother, still living at home with the old folks, didn't want to move to the Westbank. Mother did. She felt that being nearer to me would be wise as her health was going downhill fast. After her release, she came here for me to help take care of her. Remarkably, we learned that the house at the end of our block was for sale. It was a perfect house for them. It was brick like their house in Metairie, had three bedrooms, two baths, a larger kitchen than I have here, a great living room, again much larger than mine, and a huge, detached workshop in back that would be big enough for Daddy's machines when he finally retired. They had paid the loan and now owned the house in Metairie and had put a fair amount of money in the bank. If they sold their house, they would not have to worry about money for the rest of their lives. As we discussed the possible ramifications of Mother's decision to move, I began to realize Mother was unusually concerned with what would happen to my brother. She would obsess over his welfare instead of her own. No amount of reason could convince her she and Daddy should come first. Since Sammy didn't want to move to the new house, Mother insisted he needed a house for himself. She had made up her mind they would sell their house to my brother. Over my extreme protests, they got a lawyer to draw up papers selling the house to my brother for the amount they had paid 20 years before. If that wasn't enough, the "loan" was interest free. Rightly or wrongly, I felt betrayed. Her reason for moving was based on her fear that she would need me to care for her but she couldn't see she needed to be financially sound as well. My protests only resulted in her getting her back up and refusing to discuss any alternatives. In the end, they bought the house down the block and moved in on Mother's birthday that year. Our relationship was never the same. We were no longer friends and my mother and I never reconciled. We were no longer a family. At Mother's death, her children barely spoke to one another.

By the time I left work for good that day, my daughters were already living down the street. Mother had been in a home for some time before passing away and Daddy was living with my sister in Mississippi. With Mother and Daddy gone, the house had stayed empty for some time but, with the girls living there, at least it wasn't falling into disrepair. I walked into my house, sat down and felt the most complete relief. I could do anything I wanted to now. I could rest up, get my wits back and have the time to get my house in order again. It had been a long time since I had really been in charge of things around here. It was time to do some major cleaning and organizing. I was good at organizing now that I had learned all of the skills of a good secretary. I had all of the office equipment I needed. One of my bedrooms I had already converted into a completely functioning office. When I had left the last brokerage firm, I brought home all of my office machines and supplies and set these up to handle our own business and financial needs. Now I had the time to do some repairs to our financial life.

Under the circumstances, that didn't take long. Gary started taking on more and more hours at work. He lobbied for raises whenever he could. I applied every penny to what was left of our bills and in seven years, we would be out of bankruptcy. With this plan in motion, and after my house was in order, I still had time on my hands. I began gardening again. I had tried gardening a long time before, sometime in the 1980's, but it hadn't worked out. Mainly because I had three little kids and I was so depressed that nothing at that time seemed to work out for me. Now I was in much better shape, I wasn't clinically depressed, the kids were grown and gone which meant I had lots of time on my hands.

I had started watching HGTV every day. Their programming was excellent and motivating. With

Gary behind me cheering me on and supplying lots of muscle, I put up some fantastic raised beds. My entire backyard was filled with beds either on the ground or up on legs. During the time we were gardening, we grew tomatoes, squash, spinach, bell peppers, potatoes, peanuts, carrots, kohl rabbi, corn, rutabagas, collards, cucumbers, mint, dill, rosemary and probably more that I have forgotten about. I became a growing fool. One year my corn grew to well over 14 feet and was a glorious sight. At one point, I decided to grow oranges. We planted a Louisiana Sweet orange tree, a Satsuma tree, a navel orange tree and a lemon tree. We also tried pears and peaches but we were never able to produce any fruit on them. My oranges are all that is left of my original garden.

The summer of 1997, Gary had his first gastric bypass. He had finally reached a point in which his weight was beyond his ability to handle. At over 500 pounds, he had sleep apnea, was a borderline diabetic and the pain in his hips was constant. He was starting to have trouble at work. Bonnie had met someone who had the surgery and introduced him to us. He told us about his doctor and we made an appointment for a consultation.

The medical policy we had at that time approved the surgery and, on July 2, 1997, Gary had the surgery. Of course, you know that there was a great deal of work involved between the first meeting and the surgery but Dr. Martin's office worked with us and everything went as smoothly as possible. As I write this, it is hard to believe it all happened so fast. I could have sworn that it took longer from November 1, 1996, the day I walked out of work and the day Gary had his bypass but it hadn't. His recovery went well, he lost weight and the following year he had his next surgery. This one was to remove the excess skin left behind after his extreme loss of weight. Before this second surgery, Gary developed a severe case of ulcers in which he nearly bled to death. Gary is a stubborn man. He had developed a taste for Alka-Seltzer when he was a boy. He loves the fizz. Left alone, he will drink this like soda pop. After his gastric bypass, he had the usual trouble with certain foods that most people do. A no-no for all bypass patients is *NO ASPRIN*. Alka-Seltzer is fizzy, liquid aspirin. No matter how I begged, he insisted he needed Alka-Seltzer to help comfort his new digestive distresses. He didn't have to listen to the doctors' advice, he was invincible. His stubborn insistence landed him in the emergency room throwing up blood. He had to leave work that day and go straight to West Jeff hospital. That is where I found him. I had been out shopping for an aspirin free Alka-Seltzer and had actually purchased it. I got home to find a voicemail message from Gary telling me to come right away to the hospital that he was in trouble. This was back in the day before we all had cell phones. I dropped everything and rushed to West Jeff to find him propping himself against a wall waiting in a line to give the hospital his medical information. He was as pale as a ghost. As soon as he saw me, he collapsed to the floor. Hospital personnel bumped him to the head of the line for an emergency room cubical leaving me to give all the necessary information to the girl behind the counter. I got to his cubical soon after. Thus began a tug of war between this hospital and University Hospital in New Orleans over who was going to treat him. Because of where his gastric bypass had been performed, West

Jeff did not want the responsibility, his doctor wasn't on staff at this hospital so West Jeff wanted to transfer him by ambulance to University where he'd had his surgery. With Gary's doctor notified, he began coordinating with the doctors who were trying to get an ambulance sent from University. Without going into great detail, I will tell you we went through a harrowing 24 hours during which Gary lost so much blood that he nearly died. He was bleeding internally and passing it rectally. He wanted to get up and go to the toilet but it was impossible. I collected four bedpans full of blood. By late that night, and my constant protests that he was dying, it was finally determined, if he left the ER in the finally released ambulance, he would not make it to University Hospital and would indeed die. A new gastroenterologist was assigned to consult on the case. By this time Gary's blood pressure was nearly zero, he could not sit up, much less stand. He told me later, before he passed out, he was seeing stars floating around the lights in the room. Once the gastric surgeon was on board, he quickly assessed the situation, Gary was rushed into an operating room, and the bleeding ulcer was cauterized. The doctor later told me he had put the pictures of Gary's ulcer on his wall of fame at home denoting it with the dubious distinction of being the largest he had ever seen.

Gary's next surgery, the skin removal surgery, came roughly six months later. He had lost more than 200 pounds. This time he would not have to settle for University Hospital as he had for his bypass. University was a type of charity hospital. He had to be there because other hospitals worried about the failure rate of bypass patients. Many of the worst cases were not allowed at private hospitals for fear they would die, frankly. However, now that he was of a normal weight, St. Charles General would allow him the privilege of having his surgery there for the skin removal. He did not do well after this operation but not because of his weight or the hospital. After his discharge, he developed a pocket of fluid under his flesh that would continuously fill for months. We would regularly go into Dr. Martin's office to have this fluid removed only to have it fill again. The doctor would use a huge hypodermic needle and syringe to draw off the fluid. Toward the end, the doctor opened a small portion of the incision, he inserted a packing, and told me how to keep it open and draining at home. Gary continued to lose weight but now he would have bouts of high fever. At no time did he stop working. Finally, on New Year's Day 1999, the surgery sight engorged with infection and him running a high fever, we rushed to the emergency room of St. Charles General Hospital. I called Dr. Martin, he met us there and this would be where he and I cleaned out the wound site together. Dr. Martin was on one side of the gurney while I was on the other. We both worked for nearly an hour cleaning out the enormous amount of infected blood and puss that had built up inside Gary. It was drastic and had caused him to drop weight to the point that he was now down to 171 pounds. Are you wondering why I was with the doctor and not a nurse? The only nurse I saw wasn't able to handle the sight and smell. It wasn't the first time I would have to deal with a situation that a nurse couldn't do, or would refuse to do, and it may not be the last.

Our next hospital stay would come this same year. That summer I fell over the peach tree in our front yard and broke my ankle. We were just getting over all of the difficulties of Gary's surgeries and now it would be my turn. As I said, it was summer and we had decided we needed new gutters on our home. We were trying to save some money by taking down the gutters ourselves. After removing the gutters, we needed to clean the boards before installing the new gutters. The afternoon of my accident, I decided to clean the boards of all the dirt and trash that was left behind when we removed the gutters. With the garden hose stretched out across the yard, I began spraying the boards with a mixture of soapy water and got them as clean as possible. When I was done, I began to roll up the hose by pulling the hose toward the fence where the hose holder was hanging. As I backed up, pulling the hose with me, I forgot about my little peach tree just behind me. As my heel caught in the rubber dam we had around the base of the tree, I lost my balance and fell back against the tree. I heard the snap of my ankle as I fell. There I lay in the middle of my front yard unable to get up and go for the phone to call for help. Repeatedly I tried to pull myself through the grass but I was in so much pain and just too fat. Finally, a neighbor passed by in his car and asked if I needed help. He went inside my front door, found my purse and I was able to call Gary using my cell. Gary called an ambulance. I now have a plate, eight screws and six pins in my right ankle. When I woke up from the surgery, still groggy I barely remember having a phone put in my hand. Someone was speaking to me telling me that my father had died. He had been living in a VA nursing home in Mississippi. Barely out of the hospital, I attended his wake only briefly but was unable to endure the pain in my ankle to attend the funeral.

My gardening days were over. After breaking my ankle, I wasn't able to walk for some time. At first, I used one of my office chairs to roll around the house. Getting to the bathroom was the worst. Bonnie stayed with me most days. She and Gary were my biggest help. I couldn't move around very much so most of my time was spent watching television and eating. I gained a lot of weight. I have never been a strong person but, now I had lost what little strength I did have. When I was back on my feet again, I had psychically changed so much that I would never be able to garden again. When I fell, I weighed about 185 pounds. I was now over 200 pounds and I have yet to get under two hundred again.

Both of my parents were both gone now. It was time to settle their estate. Shirley, Sammy and I decided to sell the house on Rennes Drive to Rhonda with the proceeds divided equally between the three of us. We split what was left of their savings as well. Gary and I were finally in a better financial situation. With my inheritance, and the fact that we had finally learned how to manage money, we haven't had to worry about losing our house or bill collectors again.

I got fat, really fat. Gary had lost a great deal of weight and some of it I found. After breaking my ankle, I was restricted to mostly sitting or hobbling around for weeks. I couldn't get into the garden. I ate too much and did nothing to work off the extra calories. It didn't take long to start putting on the pounds. Gary started finding his lost fat too. Now we finally fit again. We went from two good-looking young people to two middle aged, fat and wrinkled boomers. Father Time is an SOB from hell and life isn't a bowl of cherries either.

I still had time on my hands. I was bored just sitting around with nothing interesting to do. As I said earlier, I enjoyed watching HGTV. In addition to gardening, they also having crafts and sewing in their programming, and I decided to start sewing a bit. My old sewing machine began giving me problems, so I decided to bring it in to be fixed. Through a series of bizarre twists and turns, I became the proud owner of a new, computerized embroidery machine. What did I know about embroidery? Nothing. However, what I did know was I was smitten the moment I saw the little machine stitching that first design.

I had walked into a small sewing center to buy a new sewing machine. I met Stephanie the sales lady. As she was putting in my order, I turned around and saw my *Baby* and I was hooked. Before the machine had even entered my new "sewing room", I already knew I wanted to create my own embroidery designs. I could see myself learning how to use the machine, learning how to put the designs on clothes, etc. and then learning how to use the software it takes to make the designs. As I would come to realize, all of the skills I had acquired since my *VO TECH* days would come into play in the next couple of years.

When you fail miserably, you wonder what it was all for. I had wondered that many times since leaving the work force. Why had I learned all of those computer programs? Would I ever use much of the financial junk I had learned? Selling cars had been a big waste of time. All of the internet skills I had, what was I going to do with all of that? All of the English classes and writing exercises seemed to be an enormous waste of time. However, only one class can I now say was an absolute waste of time, shorthand. I will never use that again. Ugh! It is amazing how much of the work I thought had been wasted effort became useful, even vital, to my future once I had purchased the little embroidery machine.

I bought the machine in the fall of 2002. One of my first challenges was to learn to use it. I took a few classes at the sewing center where I bought it. I found out rather quickly that this was going to be an expensive hobby. I would need to buy so much more just to be able use it. There were backings, toppings, clippers and tweezers, bobbins, sprays, cutaways, tearaways, and that isn't even mentioning the different color threads I would need to buy. Thread colors are at the heart of machine embroidery. You just can't have too many colors. Before I learned how to make my own designs, I would need to have stock designs. These are designs already made by someone else. You cannot stitch a design unless you have the embroidery design file to put into the machine. I found myself collecting designs. There is no way I could tell you how many hours I have spent on the internet looking for files. I discovered how to find all the places that offered free embroidery designs and began collecting them. I classified them and organized them in folders on my computer using my filing and computer skills. I had lots of time to spend doing all of this. The amount of stock designs I collected has grown over the years to become millions. I spent two years learning how to use my machine, as well as collecting designs, and stitching them on clothes and other items. Now I was ready to learn how to make my own designs.

Early in the spring of 2005, I purchased my first embroidery digitizing software program. I would now spend my time learning how to use it and how to create a well-digitized design. When I purchased the software, I was promised an instructor but could only pin him down for one whole session. For that reason I consider myself a self-taught digitizer.

Learning new software takes time. I knew that from my school days as well as at the various jobs I had failed at throughout my life. Sometimes, my learning curves took longer than my superiors wanted, this made me look slow. Many times, with someone looking over my shoulder, the pressure to perform would cause me to slow down so as not to make a mistake. I thought of myself as a slow worker. I couldn't afford to make mistakes but, with someone breathing down my neck, this was difficult for me. Here, at home, I didn't have anyone looking over my shoulder. No one would be breathing down my back. I could work at my own pace at something I wanted to do. By midsummer, I was creating complex designs. Many of my family and a few neighbors encouraged me to start my own business. The best part was I could do this from home. I didn't need to leave home to go to work and I was enjoying this very much. I would be my own boss.

In early August, I filed the paperwork for permits to start my little home-based embroidery business. After careful consideration, I came up with a name. My main consideration was that people see my business first before others in the phone book. I knew that our last name was unforgettable. It was memorable for two reasons. One, it is complicated, and two, it is very long. People don't forget it once they see it or hear it. Using these two criteria, I named my business Embroidery Designs and Monogramming by Linda. It worked. It stood out in the phone book and on the internet. People would see it first because it was long. It would make my ad bigger than other ads and I didn't have to pay for a bigger one. I complicated it by including the words "designs and monogramming" to the embroidery theme. Can you tell that I am an analytic type person?

Nothing in business happens overnight. With my fully equipped home office, flyers and business cards were no problem to whip together. My talents for creativeness came to the surface. With my multi-function printer, those items were no problem for me to distribute around the neighborhood and beyond. Only one little problem would get in my way. Her name was Katrina. Just as I had put all of the necessary, although perfunctory, details of a new business into motion, here comes Katrina to get in my way. To describe what followed would only interrupt my flow. Katrina stories abound and mine would only amount to a pimple on the back of a blue whale. It will suffice just to say she made a mess of our lives for a time, slowing me down, but not knocking me out.

My ad in the new phone books was finally published in October and word slowly began to spread that there was a new embroidery business in the area. Other embroidery businesses had left after the storm leaving room for me to pick up their customers. Still other firms had changed owners. Not all of their customers welcomed these new owners and they drifted my way. Katrina had done me a big favor after all. Is that you God? Over the years, the quality of my designs have improved with the challenges some of my customers have brought to me. Since my business is just me working from home, it is very tiny. My biggest advantage is I do all of the work. When a customer tells me what they want, it isn't passed on to someone else to do. If it is wrong, I did it and I take responsibility for it. I meet with every customer personally, we sit down, discuss their project and I know exactly what they want before they leave. Other companies send the work out to others and that is how mistakes happen. I try very hard not to make mistakes and look for ways to keep them from happening.

My business fills a need by taking the small things other firms can't, or won't do because they need volume to make money. I don't. My shop is a part of my home so I don't have that overhead and I don't have employee costs. I have very little waste and I know where every penny is spent. I haven't always spent my money wisely but, have learned what a wise expenditure is, and what it isn't. Since I am a digitizer, I can keep everything under my roof. Digitizing costs are extremely expensive. My average customer doesn't want or need digitizing but, if someone wants their own unique design, I can do the work and get to stretch my talents and grow from the experience. Being able to satisfy that need is how I have come to have the reputation I enjoy. I am able to create anything anyone wants. It has been a long journey, but I am finally proud of myself. Best of all, Gary and the girls are proud of me too.

Satisfaction means many things to many people. To me it is a happy customer. It is also that my husband is pleased with me and that my children are happy, healthy and loved. Nowhere is money a part of the equation. Money is the result of doing a good job that others want to pay for, but it isn't the primary reason I do my work. I love what I do however, I'll never get rich doing embroidery because I never want to grow beyond my ability to personally meet with and serve my customers.

9

Death and Regrets

We all have so many regrets. Where do I begin? After coming this far in my story, you already know many of them. Now is the time to talk of my girls. In 2005, the only one of my daughters I was speaking to was Rhonda. Bonnie and Sandra have both been married for years by this time. Each chose a man they felt was what they wanted, just as I had. No one would have said Gary was any parent's dream for his or her daughter. I picked him because I loved him. My girls picked their husbands and we had to accept that just as my parents had to accept my choice. Bonnie was the first to choose her husband.

Bonnie came into this world with all the promise of most children who live in a free society, but her parents were not rich. We were not poor, but she was not going to have everything she wanted. We didn't know that Bonnie would be our materialistic child, but she was. Living hand to mouth for most of your life would not make a materialist child very happy. She started her life as a happy child, or so I thought. She seemed to want to amuse people and make us laugh. She did funny little things, as a comedian would, and make us all laugh. This led me to believe she was happy. As she got older, those times got fewer and fewer. When she started school, she didn't seem to fit in. It seemed she couldn't play well with others. I find that expression apropos but extremely distasteful. She would go from episode to episode in her school life where she and the other kids would have issues. It was always something. She wasn't a particularly good student, in fact, she was getting poor grades. All of my girls had difficulty in school with their grades. Rhonda began badly because of Germany, Bonnie was still hyperactive when she first went to school and the same for Sandra. Each of them had their unique learning problems even though all were quite intelligent in their own way. I wasn't a good mother or I would have been able to help them more when they needed me most. During their early years, I was too depressed and into myself to know when they needed me. Now, it was too late. Bonnie would do whatever she wanted, she wasn't listening to me about anything.

She found drugs to be her way out of the misery she thought her life was in. As well as I thought I knew my girls and what they were capable of, I didn't see it coming. Of course, I didn't really know them at all. I had been too self-absorbed to know my girls. Just because I knew when they were lying most of the time, didn't mean I really knew them. I say this because I wasn't one of these moms who denied their child would do something wrong. There were many moms I knew of who did. I wasn't one of them. I knew my girls could, and would, lie about things. Not so much Rhonda, she didn't lie. Sandra wasn't a big liar but had done so occasionally, but Bonnie was a consummate liar. I was catching her in lies almost daily.

When we finally did accept that she had a drug problem, the realization opened up a torrent of events that led us all down a path none of us wanted to follow. I mentioned earlier that Gary had his first gastric bypass and that Bonnie was the one to suggest he go to see Dr. Martin. That fact would play a major role in the eventual course of Bonnie's life. Bonnie had a drug problem but she also had an endometriosis problem. Her condition was the first of my daughters to be diagnosed.

Having babies was never a problem for me. My middle name was "fertile", a true baby making machine. Making them wasn't the problem, raising them was. Eventually, endometriosis would attack all three of my babies. Whereas I was reproductively perfect, they were not. Bonnie actually had the mildest case. She received her diagnosis first as the result of a routine pap smear that came back positive for pre-cancer. This led her into the charity system. No longer on our health insurance, she couldn't afford to go anywhere else. What we didn't know was the reason she couldn't keep a job or get one with benefits. It was because she was on drugs.

Mainly, she used pain pills, but she was also fond of Xanax. All of this would come out later but, at the time, we didn't realize any of this.

A charity system, run by the government, is not supposed to be anyone's main source of medical care in my opinion. It doesn't hold up over time. Its purpose is to help people who are down on their luck and need a helping hand until they can get back on their feet. As I write this, the Affordable Care Act (aka Obamacare), is working its way through our lives as the "law of the land". It will destroy the best medical care the world has to offer and the reason is because it will eventually become charity for all. Without going into details I would rather not give, Bonnie found herself going from office to office, doctor to doctor and never getting good treatment. Her experiences were heartbreaking. If she had ever gotten a good job with benefits, or if she had ever been able to afford private treatment, maybe she wouldn't have had the operation.

The operation was my fault. As I said, Bonnie had gone in for a routine pap. She had been through the system without success until finally, after a particularly bad experience with one of the doctors, she showed up here crying bitterly that they would no longer be able to help her. The exact words the doctor spoke to her that day were "There is nothing more we can do for you." I cannot tell you the anguish it caused me and never mind what it had caused her. All of my daughters wanted children. Even as little girls they all loved babies and wanted them for themselves. Bonnie came to me that day literally crushed. I had never seen her so defeated and weak. Mentally she couldn't seem to get that part of her life together. She was not financially or emotionally capable of raising a child but, she could not accept the doctor's words. She really wasn't capable of raising a child.

My first response was to try and help my child. I called this unfeeling doctor and heard from her lips the cruelty she had inflicted on my girl. My next thought was to call on the nurse who was Dr. Martin's assistant. All I wanted was to find out if there was another way within the system that would get Bonnie the help she needed. I knew Martin worked within the charity system to help his patients who had no insurance. My idea was to see if his nurse knew of a number I could call that would lead to her getting some help. Instead, she wanted Bonnie to see Martin when we came in for Gary's next visit and let him assess the situation for himself.

We did just that. Martin told us that he would help her himself. It would be the biggest mistake of my life. I have to stop here. When we first met Dr. Martin, I didn't like him. There was something I felt wasn't right about this man. Was it experience? Was it a woman's intuition thing? I couldn't define it. Call it what you will, I had a bad feeling about this doctor and I was on the lookout for some evidence of it. However, try as I might, I could not find anything to point to that would say I was right. Gary loved him and that is saying something. Gary hadn't liked doctors for as long as I had known him, but Martin he liked. He felt Martin was doing a great job and even though there had been problems with Gary's surgeries, he didn't feel Martin had done a poor job as his doctor. As time went on, I had to admit that I hadn't seen anything I could point to that would justify my negative feelings about Martin. He had responded quickly to all of the problems Gary had. He was always there for us when we needed him. He had been more than generous with pain meds, knowing Gary wasn't abusing them and we couldn't say that about any other doctor we had ever seen. By the time we were to involve Martin in Bonnie's life, I'd had to admit I was wrong about Martin. So, now I will continue.

We sat down with the doctor and explained all of Bonnie's medical history. He listened and when we were through, he made his proposal. He would set up a date for Bonnie to be admitted to University Hospital and he would perform a surgery. If he could fix the problem, he would, but if not, he would perform a hysterectomy. This was serious and he wanted her to think about it and then get back to him. We talked all the way home that day. Gary told her to think long and hard about this but, he trusted Martin to do all he could to help her. Besides, she didn't have many other options to work with. She thought about all of the help Martin had been, how he was willing to work without any money from her, how he would get her admitted to the hospital for free and ultimately decided to do it.

Bonnie was admitted into the hospital, had the surgery and when it was over, Martin came out to tell us the results. I was totally unprepared for what he told me. He began by saying a woman like Bonnie needed to be given a procedure to convince them something has been done to help them. In truth, he told me what he had done was meant to have a psychological effect. He had removed her uterus and cervix and left her ovaries. Thus, she would now have a reason to believe she had been "fixed" and would no longer have a problem. I couldn't believe what I was hearing. I fell apart, crying bitterly. Gary was beside me but since he didn't understand "medical-eze", he could not understand why I would react the way I did. We were later to find out from a pathology report that her uterus was free of endometriosis, however, her ovaries were not. She still had the "non-existent" pain of endo and this disease would continue to work its way through her body.

This doctor had taken her perfectly good uterus and left her ovaries with the endometriosis. I will not pretend to know all there is to know about endometriosis but, the one absolute fact is the disease feeds on estrogen. Leaving her ovaries would leave the fuel that allowed the disease to spread. She sued him. It was malpractice and she received a settlement but ultimately it destroyed her. The seven years of fighting this doctor, along with the seven years of drug abuse that followed her surgery, took their toll on Bonnie's body and mind and she passed away on December 6, 2007 of a drug overdose. My poor baby was gone. She had so much promise when she came into this world, but left us without ever accomplishing it. She was only 34 years old.

Rhonda and Sandra have the same disease and have suffered infinitely more than Bonnie did. Each of them had more severe cases and has had multiple surgeries over the years. Both had insurance that allowed them to have access to better care, but their endometriosis was much worse. Of the three of them, I truly believe Bonnie had the best chance of a cure. I hesitate to say which one of the other two had the more severe case, but my gut tells me Sandra was worse off, but not by much. Each has suffered a great deal of physical pain, but Sandra has had more surgeries either to burn out the adhesions or remove bits and pieces of her reproductive system. As of last year, she finally had her last ovary taken to make her total hysterectomy complete. She kept hoping not to have everything removed but the endo kept coming back each time so the last ovary had to go. On top of this, she suffers with IBS and possibly IC. Understandably, she would prefer never to see doctors again. Over the years, some of her doctors were not very understanding of her condition.

Rhonda had to convince one doctor to do a scope before he would believe she even had the problem. It is a hideous disease made more so by doctors who doubt their word when a woman comes to them begging for help. After having multiple surgeries herself, Rhonda is still hanging on to her uterus and one lone ovary in the hope of someday having a child. She is now 44. The possibility is there, but only time will tell if she is ever to have a child.

10

Rise of the Tea Party

I have cast only two votes in my life that I can now say I am proud of. They were both for Ronald Wilson Reagan. There are some votes I guess I would say I had no other choice but to make. You know that old tired expression "the lesser of two evils". This kind of choice was one of the worst votes I have ever cast. I voted for Reagan of my own free will and I say that proudly. After the disastrous term of Jimmy Carter, I never again voted for a Democrat for president or any office for that matter. Both of our families were raised as southern Democrats. My family and Gary's family were all Democrats. His grandmother was active in local politics supporting all of the local heavyweights of her day. They were able to help her with social aid when she needed it most. As a single, middle-aged woman, after raising her own children, she found herself with two little boys to care for, so she needed all the help she could get. After all of that, grandma was tough, she was a survivor and would not go down without a fight. If politics would be her way to survive, then so be it.

My family had no political connections that I can ever remember hearing about. I think Daddy hated politics. I can remember him saying things like the United "Snakes" of America or that "FDR was an SOB". I know he hated Roosevelt but I didn't know why. I have no idea how he felt about Ike or JFK. I do remember I personally did not like Johnson, but it had nothing to do with his policies at the time because I didn't know his policies. I just didn't like him. What I saw of him made me uncomfortable and he looked like a lying snake to me. His wife was also a disagreeable looking woman. She looked mean, like many of my grade school teachers. That was the extent of my political knowledge when it became time for me to cast me first vote.

We spent the Nixon years in Germany. Much of the news concerning the Watergate affair came filtered through the lens of military life. President Nixon was our Commander in Chief. We couldn't see how the break-in was that big of a deal to bring down the President. Once we were back in the States and settled in as civilians, we decided to register as Democrats just as our parents had been and we dutifully voted for Jimmy Carter. He reminded me of my family in Florida. I could easily see him sitting at a dinner table with my country family of farmers drinking iced tea and eating fried chicken, biscuits with gravy, field peas with okra and a warm peach cobbler for desert. He was a good Christian man who would be a good decent President. I didn't think he would be so weak though. After giving up the Panama Canal, would he also allow those poor hostages to rot in Iran? How could he be so weak? Maybe he just didn't understand what it meant to be the leader of the free world. Maybe Miss Lillian was right, maybe Jimmy's brother Billy was the smart one. I'm being facetious of course. Need I remind you of

"Billy Beer"? The man was an idiot. Perhaps the whole family were idiots. If we consider what Carter has been up to since leaving office and some of the statements he has made around the world, it is easier to believe he is an idiot than the other possibility that he is deliberately undermining our country in the rest of the world.

When Ronald Reagan came along, we bolted to the Republican Party. Here was a strong leader. He had fire and he knew what being an American was. After the Carter years, President Reagan made me feel safe again. He wasn't perfect, but we seemed to be back on the right path after much too long on the wrong road. I didn't know anything about socialism or progressivism. I did understand Communism and what the fight with Russia was all about but, as long as we had a leader like Reagan, we would be fine. Then along came George Bush, Mr. *"READ MY LIPS"* Bush. I voted for him but never dreamed he would fall for the Democrat lies and "blink" like that. If I had known his true politics were progressivism, I would not have voted for him either. Then there was Bill Clinton, *Slick Willy*, the man from *HOPE*.

I was working downtown for the brokerage firm at that time and actually heard the term *Slick Willy* from some of the brokers we had working in our Little Rock office. They knew all about him and had a great deal to say which wasn't in the papers. I won't go into the whole Hillary healthcare thing, or the Monica blue dress stuff. We have all heard more than enough of that and you don't need me to tell you again.

The nation now turned to George W. Bush. Needless to say, "*W*" looked a great deal better than his dad after 8 years of Clinton. He seemed more like Reagan than his dad did. That's what I thought at the time anyway. At first, I was satisfied. He seemed to understand his job was a serious one, unlike Clinton who seemed amused by the whole *leader of the free world* thing. Clinton had spent eight years having a good time at our expense. Not George, he seemed to know this was serious. Then 9/11 happened and everything changed. We were at war and I was definitely glad Gore wasn't the president. Gary and I had no problem with going after Saddam Hussein. Weapons of mass destruction were there. Everyone seems to have forgotten the line of heavy trucks leaving Iraq shortly before the war. We watched them live on television as they crossed the border. What would Saddam be doing with all of those trucks except to get rid of the evidence before we got there to find it? People have short memories and the press have an agenda that doesn't include the *truth*.

We, Gary and I, voted to re-elect Bush without hesitation. The country needed a strong leader who would stand for our freedoms around the world. Kerry was a dope who couldn't make up his mind if he was for something or against it. Then, in Bush's second term, he seemed to lose his way. He somehow had turned into his dad. In the end, the liberals had him on the ropes and he lost his nerve. We got *TARP*, a bad idea from the start. I knew as soon as it hit the news this was not the way. I had been in finance and knew bailouts were never the answer. I didn't care that all of the talking heads were saying it would be the end of the world without *TARP*. Gary tried to convince me of this and would shake his head that I just didn't understand. In the end though, I was right. History will prove, if it hasn't already, that I was right. The "system" isn't better off, the American People aren't better off and the political animals feeding at the trough of *TARP* have made an even bigger mess than before *TARP*. In the middle of the "end of the world if we don't" debate, was the election contest. I had to hold my nose to vote for McCain. He was a joke. Couldn't we get anyone better to run? I can see now that the "political machine" made him the Republican candidate, not the people. We didn't have a chance.

The "machine" for the other side made theirs as well. They went all out. It was as if they went to Hollywood's central casting, found the most "perfect looking" black family they could, one that would look the best in an 8 by 10 glossy, and said "This is the one. This fellow will fit nicely in the history books". The story line was great, the look was great, they could make of him what they wanted and the American people would love it. They wrote the right script, took the right pictures and end of story. The press ate it up. Hillary who?

Out of nowhere came Barak. It didn't matter that his mother was a radical or that his father was a socialist. That his grandparents who raised him were socialist never became an issue. The mainstream media never mentioned the fact that his mentor, Frank Marshall Davis, was a Communist. The press loved him and all was sunshine and lollipops, they had their history making event and a one-dimensional character for a President. Only thing is, Obama isn't one-dimensional. He is a multi-talented, multi-dimensional disaster who's one thought is to bring down the United States, and he has the "machine" behind him, and the press to cover him while he does it. Most of the American people have no clue what is going on and may not even care. I understand the sentiment because there was a time I didn't care either. I was too busy living my life to know what was happening. I didn't know the gravity of my disinterest until after Obama took office and began the dismantling of the country, or as he calls it, the *fundamental transformation*.

Soon after taking office, Mr. Obama cranked up his engine of destruction by unleashing healthcare and stimulus. The Democrat controlled congress and senate did his bidding and rolled out insult after insult until some of us couldn't take it anymore. *The Tea Party* was born.

Gary had listened to Limbaugh for years and he would share his ideas with me. I couldn't agree with everything Rush said, but some of it I did. I had come across a few voices that made sense like O'Reilly and Hannity. However, Sean was too religious for me, and after a while, O'Reilly was beginning to get on my nerves by giving the *benefit of the doubt* too much to Obama. I found O'Reilly had a lofty opinion of himself. He seemed to have a contradiction of ideas. On the one hand, he talked of looking out for the folks, then on the other would vehemently defend the idea that no one deserved the death penalty. He saw Obama as a good man who was just uninformed or misguided. Gary and I had a habit of watching various people on all the stations and I had seen this one person on CNN a couple of times who made some sense, but I couldn't figure out what he was doing working at that liberal looney bin. Both Gary and I questioned how he ever got on CNN.

Listening to the big three networks was hopeless. I grew up with CBS, NBC and ABC. CBS was my preferred network and Walter Cronkite was, in our minds, the voice of truth. However, Walter was gone and we were not getting real news any longer. Most of cable news was worse but, FOX News at least, kept you informed on what was going on with some degree of truthfulness. We had switched to listening to FOX sometime during the Clinton years. One afternoon I saw that guy, the one from CNN. He had switched to FOX. This fellow Glenn Beck was actually saying something. He sounded like me. Most of what he was saying was right on the money. He was as angry as I was about what was happening to our country. As I continued to watch, he came up with facts and documents from history showing how things had started to go wrong. He was starting to make me think of an old TV show I used to love to watch called "Connections". This old program fascinated me to no end. If you have never seen it, it went something like this: This British fellow would start with let's say an ancient plow, and pose the question as to how that led to the discovery of rocket fuel. I'm just making that bit up, of course, but you get the picture. Well, that was what Glenn Beck was doing, filling in the missing pieces in history that the progressives hadn't wanted us to know. The more I watched, the more I learned about history and our country.

Glenn became a regular in my life. Once I had found his afternoon television program, I realized he had a radio program as well. I wasn't a radio person. Our main form of entertainment has always been TV. Gary and I are *big* TV and movie people. Since I was a little girl, I have been into TV and movies and once even dreamed of being a great actress. I would watch old movies and think I was the girl in the movie. My all-time favorite was and still is "It's A Wonderful Life". I used to watch it over and over every year around Christmas learning nearly every line of dialogue. One year Gary and the girls even made my Christmas presents all about the movie. I received the tape of the movie and a book about the making of it. I was thrilled. Most of the people I knew back then hadn't even heard of this little movie. But as time went on, this classic has actually made a comeback. Why? I think there are many reasons but mostly because it speaks to the human heart. We can all be George Bailey if we would just realize what is most important in life and trust in God. Getting back to the radio though, as I said, I found out Glenn was also a radio personality who came on locally from 9 to 11 in the morning followed by Rush Limbaugh. Of course, I wasn't very big on Rush. Gary had been listening to him forever. There was a time when I loathed the constant references Gary would make to what Rush said about this or that...now it was his turn as I began to listen to Glenn and tell him what Glenn had said.

My daily routine now changed. Gary left for work early each morning as usual but I would hurry to do as much as possible of the orders for my customers so that I could listen to Glenn. At some point, I realized I was missing an hour of his morning broadcast. He actually began broadcasting at 8 AM central time but our local station didn't pick up the feed until 9. I was missing a whole hour of information. I decided to sign up for a subscription to GlennBeck.com so that I could watch the whole show online. I linked my computer to my big screen TV and watched Glenn and the guys every morning from 8 until 11. I still do watch on my big screen but now I do it on the new Blaze TV, Glenn's network, on Dish as well as the internet on Roku. I learned so much about our country's past and about the founders and about God from Glenn. Yes, I learned about God from Glenn Beck. He speaks about God and his faith a lot. This was a problem for me for years.

At first, I would just ignore his regular references to God and how God has blessed our country and how our founders based our laws on the bible and God's laws He gave to man. I didn't want to hear the God stuff but, try as I might, it was still there. Soon after signing up and getting used to my full daily dose of Glenn, I began having an internet connection issue. I tried everything I knew to do and finally, out of total frustration, I picked up the phone and did something I had never done before. I called the show. As I said, I was not a talk radio groupie. The most surprising thing about this call was how easy it was to get in. That first morning the phone began to ring and after perhaps eight or nine rings a chipper voice said "Glenn Beck who's this?" That was the first time I had ever heard the voice of Keith.

Keith Malinak. Keith is Glenn's call screener. I believe I can at this point in my life call him *friend* even though we have never met. That first call was frantic as I tried to explain to him how I was unable to access the internet feed to the show. Not to get bogged down in the retelling of how I got to know Keith, I will just say he was kind and patient with this woman who just wanted to watch the program and, as it turned out, there were issues at that time with their equipment that would cause problems with getting the show online. For a short time, I became Keith's way of knowing there was a problem and he would in turn tell someone, somewhere that there was a glitch and it would get fixed. I felt good about being like a *town crier* alerting my friend there was trouble. There came a day when Keith totally shocked me by recognizing me by my voice alone. I didn't have to say "Hi Keith, it's Linda from Louisiana" anymore. All I have to say now is "hey" and he knows it's me and his reply is "Hey Linda, what's going on?". It was quite a while before I had a reason to call and ask if I could speak to Glenn. As it turned out, I didn't have to ask Keith. When I told him what was on my mind that day, he told me he was going to put me on hold and gave me *the instruction speech* that I know so well now.

I worked up the courage that morning to call and give Glenn the many reasons I thought he should run for President. When Keith heard my thoughts he immediately decided to put me on hold to go on the air. For some time I had been looking for anyone who could be another George Washington but there was no one. No one was a rock solid constitutionalist who understood small government and individual freedom. We are in trouble and no one is coming to save us from the trouble we are in. I had my notes in my hand. I heard Glenn say "Let me go to Linda in Louisiana" and with my heart in my throat, I began to speak. At first my nerves had me shaking so that I thought my voice would crack but I held steady. I was surprised just how much I was able to get out. I knew from listening to the show that others had been cut off mid-sentence sometimes and I held on for the click I hoped would not come. It didn't and I found he and I actually had a real conversation. As I listed my reasons why I thought he was the closest thing I could see to George Washington, he was actually making notes. Once I was finished, he launched into his reasons why he would not be the right guy. Before he was done, he was in tears and finally the call ended and he broke for a commercial. Unfortunately, my call had unintentionally brought him to tears and I sat there looking at the screen of my TV and cried bitterly for about half an hour. I know Glenn is naturally a crier but I had never intended to be the catalyst for his tears. I have spoken to Glenn a couple more times but he didn't know I was the same Linda from that first call. I met him once at a book signing in 2010 when he and O'Reilly came to New Orleans for their Bold & Fresh tour. I also had an opportunity that same day to have a brief conversation with Tania, Glenn's wife, where I sincerely apologized to her for my part in causing him to break down. She probably thought I was nuts but in my mind I believe I would not like it if someone were to cause my husband to break down so I felt the need to clear my conscience. As I think back now, I realize that all the time I spent listening to Glenn, God was dropping bread crumbs at the feet of my starving inner child and feeding my conscience along the way so that, at some point, God was going to hit me over the head with a two by four and wake me up. He used Glenn Beck's witness and my love of country as the lure to catch my attention.

I did love my country. I do love my country and I don't want to see it destroyed. The more I learned from Glenn, the angrier I got. I wasn't as angry at the people who had done this as I was with myself for allowing it to happen, or for being fooled into sleeping through the whole thing. I started to hear names I hadn't heard in 40 plus years like Bill Ayers, that dope. I heard new names like George Soros coupled with the Clintons, and how they have made plans that have little to do with the people, but more to do with their own desire to rule the world. It's one thing to hear Glenn tell of plans to institute a "New World Order" but, to hear Soros in his own words say it, that really hits home. While giving all the details he had uncovered, Glenn would challenge, "Look it up and do your own homework." I did. He was right. Sure, some of his hour-long shows were spiced with silliness, like pretending to slowly boil frogs or wearing lederhosen, and then there was his caricature of a pipe smoking elite, but I understood why he did this. These antics were used to break the tension of the dire consequences of what was being done to destroy our country. There were also times when he was so emotionally involved he would break down into tears, but he was still right. He had done his homework and we were in serious trouble as a country. The progressives had so infiltrated the fabric of our government that it was going to be nearly impossible to get us out of this mess. As time went on, I began to purchase more and more books in order to learn how all of this had happened.

I began to see the past differently. The lessons in school that were a part of my education had actually been designed not to teach the truth but to confuse us as to our true past and the founding of our country. Progressives, going back to Wilson and even Teddy Roosevelt, began to subvert the country's laws and were growing government beyond what it should be. In order for their plan to work, the people would need to be "guided" into believing this new way was good for them. Little by little, these ideas were creeping into the schools without notice, never being challenged by anyone. Now, it seems, these progressives believe the time is right for the United States to be transformed and the right person has come to do it. "No, not on my watch." This would be the cry of the Tea Party.

The summer of 2009, I went to my first and only town hall meeting. Many of us did so because of the healthcare debate. I was there for that too, but also because of stimulus, TARP, a VAT, Cap and Trade and so many other issues all coming in at once. There were so many disastrous agendas being put forth that it was overwhelming. Our little family was under assault along with the entire country, our very way of life was under threat. To add insult to injury, here was Nancy Pelosi on national TV sneering at us calling us astro-turf. I begged to differ. At our local town hall hosted by one of our U.S. Senator's, namely Mary Landrieu, I brought something to demonstrate just how much I differed. Before going that day, I dug up a clump of good ole Louisiana soil from my back yard along with genuine green grass and put it in a gift bag. After the town hall was finished, I took my bag, marched up to the dais, handed it to Ms. Landrieu and told her to tell Nancy Pelosi and all the rest of them we were not astro-turf, but real grass roots, and here was the grass to prove it. She took the bag, but my words fell on deaf ears. The vacant smile and empty look in her eyes said it all. She didn't give a fig for what I said and wouldn't even look in the bag. I feel certainly my little bag of grass went unceremoniously into the nearest trashcan.

I haven't wasted my gas or my time going to town halls anymore. When asked to call my congressional representative or senators, I will if I feel like it, but I know it doesn't do any good, especially with Ms. Landrieu. I have a magnet on my car that says it all. With the capitol as a backdrop the caption reads: "Throw the bums out."

My time has been spent going to a few local Tea Party meetings, but more importantly, we have participated in the rallies for 9/12, Restoring Honor and Restoring Love. Thanks to Beck and his 9/12 Project, we know we aren't alone and, even if we lose this battle or that battle, we are confident that we are standing for what we know is right. I have a Facebook page and a Twitter account but don't use either one. Lately though, I have begun to think that we baby boomers need to get with it. We need to start using these new mediums to express our displeasure. The people representing us are not listening at town halls anymore, they don't open our letters, they don't take our calls and they ignore our emails and faxes. However, when a news story or event goes viral on the internet, they pay attention. This new medium makes news like no other and it is nearly instantaneous. We who love our country as founded, who don't want it transformed into a socialist "utopia", need to learn how to use these tools to reverse the tide of insanity that is the *Obamanation*.

Our household income was a great source of pride for Gary. He would tell you himself that he would worry, as a boy, how he would support a family. Not having a male role model to guide him, he didn't do well in school. His grandmother didn't see education as a priority in his life and his formal education went only to the fourth grade. When we got married, he had no trade. It took the military to give him a way to support his family. Throughout the years since leaving the military, our income had steadily risen. Most of the time, the rising amount would be absorbed by either an increase in the size of our family, inflation or our own poor decisions. It wasn't until after Katrina that we truly began to see our income become a way of adding to our wealth.

We finally became able to save cash on top of the automatic 401-k payroll deductions. We felt good seeing our bank statements and our retirement portfolio grow. Gary began to feel as though he was finally a success as a provider. While we were "Katrina refugees", he learned his value to the company he was working for. He had been an important asset to the business all along, but he hadn't realized it. After Katrina passed, he found that other companies were willing to pay him more than he was getting at Deltide. He realized how important he was to his company. Did he leave the company who had treated him as a less than valuable member of their team for over twenty years? Did he tell them to shove the job that had ruined so many holidays? Did he say good bye to the manager who had insisted that he stay in the storm's aftermath and take care of the building that had been ravaged by Katrina and wasn't fit to stay in, who demanded that he stay while bullets were flying around him? No, he did not. He asked for a raise. Those in charge knew he had been approached by another company, but he remained loyal. Repeatedly, whenever he had asked for a raise, he was told they couldn't afford it. But now he knew what he was worth and they weren't able to deny him any longer. Unfortunately, in 2009, the fishing tool company he had been with for over 25 years decided to sell out to a big corporation. I knew this wasn't good. Since working for corporations before, I knew how impersonal they are. The rules were going to change with this new development. In all the years Gary had worked for Deltide, he didn't have to concern himself with cameras and time clocks or badges and security guards. His every move wasn't monitored and recorded by the corporation. This, however, would change. In early 2010, they wanted him to sign some sort of corporate agreement that if he were to leave the company for any reason, he couldn't work in his field for a year or some such nonsense. That would mean he couldn't make a living anywhere else but there. He wouldn't sign so he left. Shortly after, he was asked to return for a chat. I cannot prove it, but I believe the corporate bosses found that they still needed him for a little while longer. He didn't have to sign the agreement. During the few weeks between the time Gary refused to sign and his reinstatement, we believed we needed to take possession of his 401-k. Once begun, it could not be stopped. The loss was huge but we did do one good thing. We paid off our mortgage.

He returned to the company believing all was well. During that summer however, it was decided that he would be required to train others to do his job. One employee had already been under Gary's instruction for some time, but he wasn't very cooperative. This trainee would only learn what he felt like learning and no more. With an additional trainee, perhaps there would be enough welders to handle the expected increased demand coming their way. When the corporation took over, the expected demand for their services was great. In any case, a new hire was added for Gary to train. This fellow was even worse than the first. His attitude was combative and belligerent. After repeated attempts to get him to settle in to what was expected of him, Gary began to make it plain to those in charge that things were not working out. This trainee would not follow direction and refused to do what was expected. Repeatedly, Gary would go to the managers begging for them to take steps to get this fellow to do his job and take directions to learn his job, but nothing changed. After months of this, the situation came to a head on December 17, 2010. This particular morning the fellow chose to challenge Gary by saying that they would have an "incident" when Gary least expected. With a kind of evil grin, he let Gary know he may find himself in danger from this man. Gary again went to management and they refused to help. Not only did they refuse to help, but Gary was told he had no choice, he would have to work with this person. He did have a choice, he could leave the job. This was something he did not want to do, but since he worked with this man alone many times at night, he could conceivably get hurt while his back was turned. Their working conditions were such that Gary wouldn't even see it coming much less be able to defend himself. He left the job. Since then, the company found that both men Gary had tried to train were not able to do their jobs and both were ultimately fired and were not replaced. The company lost almost all of the jobs they thought they would need more workers to do. With the BP oil spill, Louisiana's oil and gas industry has suffered to the point that Gary hasn't been able to find another job. The actions taken by all that day changed our lives forever. Since 2009, I have seen Gary's self-esteem erode as he realized the only job market he is qualified to participate in has disappeared. He is now 68, there aren't any carbide jobs available and he doesn't feel able to learn a new skill. Despite the fact that he detested the job, he still felt what he did was worthwhile. He was able to support his family and finally thrive. Now, he is torn between the freedom of not waiting by the phone with the possibility of it ringing and having to leave and go to a job that was such misery, and living with the fact that it will never ring again. He was not happy before, but at least he was proud of the prosperity we enjoyed. He had accepted the fact that what he suffered was the price he had to pay for not having an education. He had only gone to the fourth grade, but he was able to learn a trade that earned him six figures.

We have actually grown closer in the last three plus years. We have spent virtually every moment together with only minor exceptions since December 17, 2010. We have learned to share our chores and have adjusted our time so that each has a say in what we do. We have had to go through a period of adjustment that, at times, has been somewhat painful, but with love and understanding, we have worked though our differences.

On March 1st 2013, the news of the day was the Democrats wanted us to believe we are going to collapse without an additional 2% increase in the federal budget. I am talking about the sequestration. Maxine Waters even had the chutzpah to say we would lose 170 million jobs without it. The trouble with this number was we did not have 170 million jobs left in the country. We *might* have had that many before Obama but we certainly do not have that many now. Since taking office, Obama has blamed a host of characters and a myriad of things as the reason our country is losing jobs and productivity. He has tried to blame Bush, the banks and the tsunami. He even has had the nerve to blame the use of ATM's for our woes. He has yet to take the blame for anything. He has used the Saul Alinsky model and seems to have out *Alinsk-ied* Saul.

We had the hope that we could stop the Obama agenda. We lost the fight over Obamacare when Chief Justice Roberts lost sight of what his role as a

Supreme Court Judge was. The only hope we had was to elect someone else. That didn't happen. If anything, instead of encouraging more people to see the need to vote, we now know that even less people came out to vote in November of 2012 than in '08. I am very sad that we can no longer count on the American people to do the right thing.

The Republican Party isn't any better. With Obama in for another term, they have decided the Tea Party is their enemy. We are too extreme and right wing. They think the middle, straddling the fence, is the place to be. Well, sitting on the fence can become more uncomfortable the longer you are there. Those boards can dig into your butt and hurt and it doesn't take very long before your butt becomes numb. They have lost sight of the truth. The Republican "machine" has drifted to the center and beyond. They are where the Democrats were during Clinton it seems to me. Weasels who only want power are still weasels whether they be Republicans or Democrats.

I would like to sum up my analogy of what is going on in Washington as a big ping pong game. On one side, you have a group of people with their paddles. Let's call them the Rodents or Roaches or Reptiles, anything unpleasant that starts with the letter "R". Next, we have a group on the opposite side of our imaginary table with their paddles and let us call them the Dogs, Demons or Despots. You see where I am going. Finally, you have the little white ball. In my game, we see both sides with their paddles smacking the little ball back and forth across the playing field. The paddles are their laws, rules and taxes. The little ball is "WE" the people. You see the "R's" and the "D's" getting elected and using their paddles to smack the "people" back and forth with these laws they make up and then hitting us with them. We the people bounce back and forth between the two parties every election, but we aren't getting any more out of this game than the ball does. While, we the people are being knocked senseless, the R's and D's are having a great deal of fun and getting richer and more powerful. All of this is causing a great deal of damage to the country. The greatest damage is the fact that the people are being played. Some of us see the game, don't like it and want it to stop. Others have no clue there is a game or that they are the little ball. Then, finally, there are those who know the game and are enjoying the game. They think this game is good for them. What they do not know is the game will not only hurt the people they feel deserve to be hurt, but it will also hurt them. This game has been going on for a very long time. It has been doing grave damage to our country. The more damage that has been done, the less likely we are to recover.

Mr. Obama, since taking office, has done nothing but borrow and spend money we can never pay back, pass laws that will cripple our economy, sign executive orders and directives to bypass congress, and bad mouth our country. Also, his Federal Reserve chairman, Ben Bernanke, who was also George Bush's Fed Chair is printing money at a rate of over $8 billion with a *B* each month. Another way of looking at this is to realize this printing is really *Monopoly Money*. It isn't real and is based on nothing real. On a personal note, my opinion of this monetizing by the Fed needs to stop and the best way is to first audit the Federal Reserve and then abolish it once and for all.

With Mr. Obama's new term underway, the rhetoric has only increased. After using the phony *war on women* issue to win reelection, we hear things like "fair share" but no one will define what that means. We hear how the evil rich have stolen the wealth from the poor, but not how they did it. If you ask any one of my customers what they want from their businesses, they will tell you they want it to grow and make them money. Some of them want to be rich. However, many of them mostly likely voted for Obama. If they were ever successful, would they not then become the very rich they have been told to hate? If their dreams were to come true, then they too would become the targets they now are told are evil and need to be destroyed.

The Republicans do not seem to have the will to do the very things necessary to right our ship of state. They whine and complain but in the end fold like a cheap suit. There have been few of them willing to stand up and do the hard job of telling the American people the truth and giving us a real choice against the current agenda in Washington. Currently, most are content to nibble around the edges of the many

"Obama" administration scandals. Obamacare has been the law of the land since March 23, 2010, but *NOT REALY* because he has dictated with his pen dozens of changes in the "law" since it took effect and even since enrollment began last fall. According to a Fox news report outlined on the show *Special Report With Bret Baier* which aired March 17th there have been 34 Obamacare delays and fixes since 2012 alone. The law itself is more than 2,700 pages long which Mr. Baier points out is itself pretty hefty. However, because of the way the law is written, the Department of Health and Human Services (HHS) has been given the dubious responsibility to write regulations which will *adjust* the law. If you add up all of the new rules and proposed regulations that have been written so far to *adjust* the law, it would add up to over 21,000 additional pages making the combined total pages to over 23,700 and counting. Adding insult to injury, the Obamacare website is a nightmare and most of the *enrollees* have been through the Medicaid system. Of the touted 7.1 million sign-ups, nearly one in three "paying" enrollees haven't actually paid their first premium. This from a law that was supposed to allow those who liked their plan and their doctor to keep what they had and would cover the 30 million uninsured in our country. Neither of these have happened, rather, over 7 million people have actually lost their plans that they were told they could keep. Instead of reducing premiums by $2500 the plan has increased costs by $2500 or more. Besides the Obamacare nightmare, the myriad of scandals include but are not limited to: "Fast and Furious", the NSA collecting data on everyone as revealed by Edward Snowden, the cover up of the deaths of our Libyan ambassador and others in Benghazi, the IRS' targeting the Tea Party and other conservative groups before the 2012 election, **Solyndra-Gate,** and targeting news reporters like James Rosen of Fox News. Just recently, Senator Diane Feinstein blasted the CIA for spying. It was widely reported that Senator Diane Feinstein (D-CA), the head of the Senate Intelligence Committee, stated on March 11, 2014 that the CIA had illegally monitored and searched computers that belong to her committee. This latest scandal seems to have even raised the ire of Democrats which frankly takes some doing. The alphabet soup of U.S. agencies willing to circumvent the laws we all believe in would make people's heads explode if they bothered to pay attention. As for the Republicans, they have not been able, or willing, to reverse the course the progressives have been setting for 100 years. I believe it will take a higher power.

11

Wake Up and Live

God is good. He gives you just what you need when you need it most. I had begun feeling something stirring inside me since 2011. With the little crumbs dropped by Glenn, my mind was unconsciously absorbing the truth of God's existence, the many ways He has used people and circumstances to bring about this country and many other miracles we weren't paying attention to. It seems to me, I began to truly notice a change in my thinking somewhere around the time I hurt my back.

We decided early on to take advantage of the Road Home Program established by the Federal

Government after Katrina. Many people, after the storm, left the area and were scattered all over the country and there were so many voices crying out for the people to return to the city and rebuild. New Orleans seemed to be dying. Opportunists had moved in looking to make the city over in their image and our local elected officials were happy to oblige. Washington decided they needed to step in. Therefore, FEMA started "Road Home" to help people rebuild. It didn't work very well, as many of us who live here can tell you. The high-minded, grandiose plans by those in Washington never produced the stated goals of Road Home, which was to provide the funds to rebuild or restore those homes which had been damaged or destroyed. What did happen was predictable. The government bureaucracy got bigger, some wealthy people close to government got even wealthier, a few people got some crumbs, and the rest are still waiting. If you want to see it play out, check out what is happening on the East coast with the Sandy survivors. It is all happening again.

Getting back to my back, as I said, we had put in for a Road Home program for people who wanted to take advantage of the elevation project. The government had worked out a program to elevate homes above flood levels in lower lying areas. We qualified, and so, with money from the government, we were having our home raised and also having shutters put on all of our windows. Shortly after the process began, I decided to temporarily shut down the business because of safety reasons. When a house is being raised, the entire house is surrounded with construction debris that make entering and leaving the house a difficult procedure. The construction site was already well underway, but shortly before I was told the house would finally be lifted off the ground, I stopped taking any more orders so none of my customers would get hurt trying to drop off an order or pick one up. It seemed the only sensible thing to do.

Now that I had officially stopped working and the house was high in the air, we decided we needed to put forth more effort into losing weight and getting some exercise. Losing weight is a constant battle for us. I told you about Gary having his first gastric bypass and his ulcers, but he had by this time had another bypass operation and I had had the surgery as well. His second surgery came because of the ulcers. His ulcers had caused so much damage that his new doctor saw the need to redo his original surgery. We had left Martin after his treatment of Bonnie and found another gastroenterologist for Gary's treatment. I had my bypass after Gary's second surgery. I had been gaining weight since I broke my ankle and now I had ballooned to a whopping 317 lbs. I knew had to do something or I wouldn't be able to function soon. Our medical insurance policy would not cover my surgery so in early 2007 we self-paid. It wasn't easy parting with $20,000 dollars but that was the only way I could get help. I began losing weight immediately and felt better than I had in years. The lowest I had gotten after surgery was 225 pounds, I think, and I had actually gained some of that back. Now, here it is summer 2011 and I had no excuse for gaining, I needed to get back to work and loose the weight. We both did.

This particular day, Gary and I were getting ready to go for our daily walk. I was eager to go because I was doing well with my weight loss efforts and wanted to keep it going. I had found an old pair of jeans I hadn't worn in years and, *WOW*, they fit. I was so very pleased with myself having lost enough weight to fit into those jeans. Feeling particularly energetic, I hurriedly put on my shoes and socks but, as I lifted my leg to put on a sock, I felt an uncomfortable stitch in my lower back. Not wanting to give in to a minor ache or pain, I ignored it. After descending the makeshift wooden stairs to our front door, we climbed into the car and I felt the need to use my hands and lift my right leg just to get it into the passenger seat. This was not good. Ok, I'm stubborn, I admit it, what can I say. I was determined to ignore my body's warning and walk it off.

Gary wasn't feeling any better himself, but he never really was into the whole walking thing in the first place. While I walked around the Bent Tree subdivision walking track, he decided to sit in the car. After only twice around the quarter mile track, I had to stop. My back was getting worse and my leg felt like lead. A shooting pain was working its way down to my ankle. I got back into the car but, still stubborn to the end, I needed groceries so we headed to Winn-Dixie for a few things. I went in, got what I needed and we left. By the time we got back home, I was in serious pain. After another hour had passed, the pain was so severe I decided I needed to call someone. Since the loss of Gary's job, I no longer have health insurance. My first call was to our doctor of record. I inquired as to what the charges would be for me to come in. Her charges were well beyond our budget now that we no longer had health insurance and our income was so low. I then decided to call a GP we had not seen for years and see what he would charge me. I was told the office visit would be under $100. He wasn't available until the next day but that was the best option for us, so I waited. The pain got worse, much worse. I spent the night in the most excruciating pain I have had in a very long time. I couldn't sit, I couldn't stand and I couldn't lie down anywhere for very long. I cried out in pain nearly all night long. Standing, sitting and lying were a process that took time to accomplish. I don't even want to describe the effort it took to do this. Needless to say, it was a sleepless night and the next day took forever to finally arrive. We got to the doctor's office before it opened. By this time, Gary was beside himself with worry. Men are like that when they are unable to do anything to help. I felt sorry for him as he wanted so desperately to do anything to relieve my pain. As we waited for my turn, the office began to fill with other patients and my constant moaning and pacing, along with my efforts to sit down or get up, were a disturbance I was unable to control. I had, by this time, run out of tears so all I could do was make these pitiful sounds of agony. My doctor was sympathetic but unable to do anything other than tell me I needed to see a back specialist. His recommendation was that I go to the Charity Hospital in New Orleans or the one in Houma. He prescribed a strong painkiller and told me I needn't come back as there was nothing more he could do.

Gary and I discussed this dilemma once we got back with the prescription and I felt sufficiently drugged. No way, we decided, would I be allowed to see a charity doctor for back surgery. It was out of the question. Back surgery was risky enough with the best doctors, but a charity doctor, absolutely not. I began searching the web for answers. I knew the pain started when I put on my shoes so I began to try to find out what would cause this kind of injury and how to help relieve the pain. I settled on seeing a chiropractor. Gary had been to see one years before who was related to his old boss, and my next door neighbor Linda had seen this same doctor as well, so I put my back problem in his hands.

When I began my treatment with the chiropractor, I had a few pain pills left but was running out fast so I called my GP's office and was given an additional 15 pills. This meant I could go maybe 3 or 4 more days if I was very careful. The Friday after my *accident* Rhonda surprised us with a visit. Gary and I were both shocked when she opened the front door and walked in. We have always been the kind of family that drops everything to come together under these kinds of circumstances, but this visit was remarkable. Unbeknownst to me, Rhonda had been given an enormous amount of pain pills and muscle relaxers by a doctor in Baton Rouge. She had been having problems of her own with pain in her hip. She has since told me she hadn't asked for pain medication, but this particular doctor just wrote the prescriptions and included 3 refills. She was swimming in them. This never happens, or at least it never happens to us. When she handed me the bottles of pills, I nearly fainted. If I had prayed for this, I would be lying. God knew I was in trouble and he used Rhonda to help me. I am now convinced of it. Even though I was, at that point, an atheist or claiming to be, God knew something was different inside me. I knew I was feeling things I could not explain. I had begun to have my doubts about there being no God, but would not admit them. The wee small voice that speaks to us was whispering in my heart, but I still would not listen. Rhonda's connection to God was all that He needed to reach me and He used it to help me when I needed it most. Those pills got me through the rest of the year, along with the chiropractor's help. Nevertheless, I didn't really see any of these signs until much later. As I said, we don't always see the forks in the road until they're past.

By the spring of the year, 2012, I am busy with work and my business is doing well. It's dawning on me that something is definitely different in my life. I find myself thinking of God more and more. Gary and I have been together day and night for over a year and haven't killed each other. We are working things out. We begin again to lose weight with a new diet that included daily shots. I am trying to do all I can do help him and myself as I know that the chances of our needing medical attention will increase with the added weight. We hadn't been back on a diet since my back problem. Sometime in May, I felt a presence so strong that I began to talk to God. If that *is* YOU, please God, let me know. My past came back to me when I used to cry bitterly for God to help me. When I got no answer, when I felt only emptiness, I decided there was no God. Now, here I was feeling God when I hadn't asked for it. It had just come to me. I didn't know this could happen. Was this really *God*? *"Wake up dummy......it's me, God, and I want you to live"* was His answer. I began to talk to God. I just talked about anything and everything. Then, early one morning, during a particularly long session of talking to God, I prayed "God, I've always wanted Wilcom to do better work for my customers, but it is so very expensive. Can you help me?"

Wilcom is the premier software for embroidery digitizers. It is a program that I have seen selling anywhere from $14,000 to more than $20,000 over the years since I first began to learn how to digitize. There is no way on earth I would ever be able to justify spending that much, especially now that Gary was no longer working. Therefore, asking for Wilcom was like asking for the moon. I am not sure if it was one day or two now. However, within days of this small timid prayer request, I found an email in my inbox from a company that distributes Wilcom saying that its full version was available for only three more days at the unheard of price of $2999, with the trade in of any other embroidery software program. *Shut up!!! This can't be for real!!!* Again, I prayed to God that, if this was what He wanted me to do, I would find a way to do it. I called the woman who owned the company and we talked it through. Yes, she said, this was a legitimate Wilcom offer and would be available through the weekend.

I went to Gary and told him about the email offer. I left out the God part though. He wouldn't believe me anyway. He knew what Wilcom meant and how much I have always wanted it. He also knew what its usual price tag was as well. Fortunately, we have no debt by this time. All of the credit cards we use, we pay off each month. As soon as the statement came though, I paid it off with some of our savings. God showed me the way and I was able to get something I had always wanted but couldn't afford before. My work is improving with this new program as I learn how to use it more and more each day.

Soon after this experience, I found I needed to see my GP again. I needed to get a new prescription for my hormones and our B-12 so I decided I would ask him for more pain pills along with some muscle relaxers like the ones Rhonda had given me. I had been nursing these since her contributions to my medicine store for use whenever we needed them. It is hard getting old and, when we had our gastric bypass surgeries, we were unable to take *NSAIDS* as they cause ulcers in bypass patients. Pain pills are necessary but are so very hard to get these days. Doctors have to be on guard for people who are addicts and those who would abuse them. My own experience has taught me just how hard it is to get them even when you are in pain. Our experience with Bonnie's addiction illustrated just how dangerous they are as well. Even so, we need something for those times that come along when we are in pain and going to a doctor isn't an option. With my bad back, knee problems and the occasional issues with my broken ankle, I made up my mind that I was going to ask him for the pills. After all, the worst he could do was say no. I made my appointment and went to his office. After I parked the car, I sat down and said a small prayer to God that if He was agreeable, if it was His will, that my doctor would agree to help me with a prescription for pain medication and muscle relaxers. I had the bottles Rhonda had given me with me so, when I asked him for the prescriptions, I could show him exactly what she had and when I got them. I won't keep you on pins and needles, he agreed and gave me a prescription for 90 of each.

When I entered the exam room, I sat down and contemplated what I would say. I had the pill bottles for the two prescriptions Rhonda had given me, the hormone bottle and the liquid B-12 as my *evidence* which I now had sitting on the table to my right. I thought back to what Rhonda had said that morning. I told her my plans and she said, "No way." She has seen this same doctor much more than I have and knows him better. She likes him a lot but knew how he was about pain meds. She warned me strongly that he would probably not give them to me, but if he did, it wouldn't be what I planned to ask for. She reminded me of the last year when I was in such agony and the small amount he had given me back. All I could say was I believed in my faith in God and He would to do the right thing. If God knew it would be wrong for me, then the doctor would say no. I didn't need to worry over this but just accept the outcome with trust in God to do what was best.

When I got home, I sat down in front of Gary and told him very calmly what had happened. With a bit of apprehension, I added that I believed that God had a hand in the outcome. I expected him to become difficult over the news of my new-found spirituality. I had seen firsthand his hostility toward God and we had shared the disbelief for too many years not to know what his reaction might be, but this day he was very calm considering the weight of the subject. His only concern seemed to be was I going to start going to church and getting all religious on him again. I don't remember his exact words but it was something to that effect. I assured him it wasn't anything like that. I told him it wasn't a religion I had gotten into, it was a feeling like God was actually present and communicating with me. "Please understand," I said, "I don't understand it myself, but I feel like God just wanted to let me know He was there and that I should trust Him that He was with me." Please, it isn't as if I expected him to fall to his knees and praise Jesus, but he didn't go all hostile on me either. He really took it quite well. His main concern was that I not change his life. This was much easier than I thought. God is good.

With this part behind me, I felt as if I now would try to find out what God expected of me and I really wanted to know God for the first time in my life. I found myself looking for answers to questions I never expected to ask. I hope you can understand my analogy here. It was sort of like when you get a paper cut. You don't usually think about your finger but, when you get that paper cut, now your attention is drawn to it and you're thinking about it all day long. Eventually, the cut heals and you go back to not thinking about your finger any longer, not so with God and me. Since He woke me up, I am always thinking of Him and Jesus and what He wants me to do. I am looking for answers to everything. I tried to remember the things I learned as a Witness, but nothing except the "hell" thing is left. I have to say, all the studying I did was for nothing. I cannot remember for the life of me anything except that "hell" is the grave. That's it. So, what does God want me to know? I wanted "meat and potatoes" information. I had to know what God wanted from me, what I was meant to do.

I came across a book that really helped a lot. It's called *The Harbinger* by Jonathan Cahn and it showed me that the word of God is alive. My suggestion is for you to get a copy and read it. I cannot recommend it highly enough. While reading this book, I could see how much trouble our country was in and how God was warning us to wake up. As long as we ignored Him, we would continue to be under threat from without *and* within. It was so very clear. Our nation had made a covenant with God when the Pilgrims arrived. Our founding fathers made their covenant and they meant for it to last forever. We were to put Him above all. They wrote our laws based on His word, but we have turned our back on Him, and with the example of ancient Israel, the writer of this book was able to show the result of our actions. I knew that this book had answers I needed and it helped me to understand why so many of the things that had happened in my own life were because I had turned my back on God. Since reading this book, I also believe I understand why God gathered together people like Washington, Jefferson, Adams, Madison and Franklin. These were men who would risk everything to break away from a country that would keep mankind from fulfilling the will of God. Our country *is* special, just as ancient Israel was special. Before America was discovered, the word of God had only gone so far. The mission of Jesus was to save the world. He told his followers to spread the word to the whole world. They were to become *fishers of men*. I have come to believe that God founded the United States to help that to happen. If you doubt this, get the book *The Covenant* by Timothy Ballard and read it. If you aren't a reader, get and watch the movie *Monumental: In Search of America's National Treasure* with Kirk Cameron. If you are really interested, do both and you will see what I mean. In order for God's word to spread worldwide, He needed a free country as a sort of base. He made sure the right people were at the right place at the right time in history. If we look at the group of men who founded our great nation, nowhere on earth were so many great men able to come together to form a better country. A country founded of the people, by the people and for the people and they asked God to bless this country. They asked for Divine protection. By contrast, we now have leaders who daily defy the will of God. Our modern day elected officials have chosen to break the law of God defiantly instead of upholding the covenant. I can see this as a mark of the end of our country if we don't fix this problem. As long as our leaders continue to break God's law and deny Him, we will be under judgment from God.

I had wasted so much time. Did I have enough left to make the necessary changes in my life to get into line with the will of God? I can only say that I will use whatever time I have left to put God first in my life and devote myself to doing His will. I continue to look to the word of God for guidance every day and hope that more people will do the same.

I don't know if I can convey with words what it feels like to have God in my life. Since those first stirrings, I can tell you I have not been alone in my skin. What I mean is I was alone in my own skin until God whispered to me to *"wake up"* and I felt His presence in me. You must know what I mean when I say I was alone in my skin. It doesn't make sense that I am the only one to feel this way. It is like being in a cocoon that is my own body. I cannot say what it is like being you or how you feel in your body, I can only know what it is like in mine and I felt alone within myself until I felt God in here with me. As I sit here writing all of this, I feel God's presence, Jesus' presence and the Holy Spirit.

Before I go on, I would like to describe how I understand the Trinity. God, of course, made everything and He has always been. Jesus is God made flesh to walk, talk, and be with us to know what being human feels like. He is also God in a form we can relate to as opposed to a spirit. In John 1:1-5, the disciple John writes: ***In the beginning was the Word, and the Word was with God, and the Word was God. ²He was in the beginning with God. ³All things were made through him, and without him was not any thing made that was made. ⁴In him was life, and the life was the light of men. The light shines in the darkness, and the darkness has not overcome it.***(ESV) John goes on in verse 14 to say ***And the Word became flesh and dwelt among us and we have seen his glory, glory as of the only Son from the Father, full of grace and truth***. Then there is the Holy Spirit. The first mention in the Bible of the Holy Spirit is Genesis 1:2 speaking of creation it says: ***The earth was formless and empty, and darkness covered the deep waters. And the Spirit of God was hovering over the surface of the waters***. When Moses took his staff and went before Pharaoh, the bible says in Exodus 7 verse 10: ***Moses and Aaron went to Pharaoh and did as the L***ORD*** had commanded. Aaron threw his staff down in front of Pharaoh and his officials, and it became a large***

snake. This to me shows that God gave Moses the ability through the Holy Spirit to do great things he was not able to do on his own. Jesus promised the disciples the same thing in John 14:15-17 *"If you love me, you will keep my commandments. [16] And I will ask the Father, and he will give you another Helper, to be with you forever, [17] even the Spirit of truth, whom the world cannot receive, because it neither sees him nor knows him. You know him, for he dwells with you and will be in you"*. One final example I would like to share is this, Acts Chapter 2, verses 1-4, **On the day of Pentecost all the believers were meeting together in one place. [2] Suddenly, there was a sound from heaven like the roaring of a mighty windstorm, and it filled the house where they were sitting. [3] Then, what looked like flames or tongues of fire appeared and settled on each of them. [4] And everyone present was filled with the Holy Spirit and began speaking in other languages, as the Holy Spirit gave them this ability**. (NLT) When I feel the Holy Spirit inside me, I am able to do things I would never be able to do on my own. I am able to understand the Bible because of God's Holy Spirit and then apply it in my life. I could site so many scriptures for these examples, but I am sure I have given you more than enough to know what I mean.

It is warm in here now where before it was lonely, or maybe I should say more like solitary. Does that make sense? Anyway, I can never know what it is like to be anyone else or truly connect with anyone else, but I was constantly trying to feel something of what others do. Before I was old enough to know better, I trusted people, I loved people and loved being with people even though they may not have wanted to be with me. It was hard for me to understand why someone would not want to be friends with me. It took time for me to realize that not everyone was as open to connecting as I was. People say children can be cruel. That is true, but adults can be just as cruel and sometimes even more so. When I learned that lesson, I decided to guard my feelings and withdrew into myself, into my cocoon. Still, I would try to put myself into another's shoes to understand what they felt. It has been my experience that getting it right was a hit or miss proposition. My analytical skills have not helped me figure out a system for understanding others well enough to stay out of trouble or get hurt. Try as I might, I still hurt the feelings of those I love and get my feelings hurt by those I love. I now understand that not being able to crawl inside others and truly know how they feel is the real reason for the pain. God knows me and I know Him because I can feel Him and He can feel me. That is the difference in me now. Even when I mess up, God knows I don't mean to. Because of the redemptive power of Jesus Christ, I know I will be forgiven for my failures.

Then there are times when something speaks to me in a warning or one of those "ah-ha" moments and I just know it came from God's Holy Spirit helping me out somehow. You just know. If I'm paying attention, if I am not being willful or stubborn, I find that those moments bring me closer to the will of God and make me a better person. Living with God is a comfort like no other. Even when I am alone, I'm not really alone. I have a warm comforting feeling inside and I know I am loved.

To understand better what I feel imagine you find yourself driving alone in your car. Further, imagine you are lost and have no idea where you are going. Suddenly, you realize you are no longer alone but the person you trust most is in the car with you. This person knows where you came from, how you got where you are now and how to get to where you want to go. Now imagine this person says to you *"Relax, I've got you covered"* and along the way He says to you He has added two more people to your rode trip to help you. These two are *His* best friends and most trusted helpers. Your car is now packed with the three most trusted people you have ever known. They know just what to do and how to do it and they are taking you just where you need to be. Your trip may take you through parts of town you'd rather not go or you may find yourself in some of the most breathtakingly beautiful scenery you have ever seen. Just as likely, however, your trip will have some of both. My car has me and all three of God's personages. First there is Jehovah-Jireh (Gen. 22:14) "The Lord our provider" who has added Jesus and the Holy Spirit to my car. No matter what happens I'm covered. Praise God and His Holy name. You don't believe it? Then try it for yourself. Begin by reading God's word then allow yourself to listen to that little voice in your head. It may be a tiny little whisper but it will grow louder. The next thing you know you will receive the warmest of all hugs from Jehovah-Raah (Ps. 23) our *Shepherd* who tenderly leads us. These three will let you know that, no matter what happens on your journey through life, you will get there safely and everything will be fine.

I do feel blessed that God would think so much of me to pull me up from where I had sat down and let me know He cared. As I began to realize the presence of God inside me, I was able to forgive myself for all of the wrongs I had done. I began to accept myself and was able to move on to forgiving others. I had not been the kind of person to hold grudges but there were sore spots in my past that had haunted me. Daddy called me "stupid", okay he was wrong, but now I can truly say, "I forgive you." The pain is gone. I have accepted the fact that forgiveness is a two way street as Jesus talked about in the Lord's Prayer: please God *"forgive our debts as WE forgive our debtors"*. On the other hand, as I like to think, "Please God, forgive me my wrongs as completely as I forgive the wrongs others have done to me." The power of forgiveness, in my humble opinion, is everything. It is the most important thing I have learned from studying God's word. There is a famous quote from the movie *'Love Story'* that says, *'Love means never having to say you're sorry'*. This is not true. Absolute love is complete forgiveness. Only God can completely forgive us.

Over and over God uses His Word in our manual, the Bible, to show us how He forgives and at the same time He gives us prophetic images of the coming of His sacrifice, Jesus, for our sinful, imperfect Adamic nature. In studying the word of God, I now see how God showed, through circumstances in the lives of others, the coming of Jesus. Sometimes I have to stop myself and say, these aren't stories, these are real people who lived. I don't know about you, but that can be a difficult concept to hang onto. Just as Adam really lived and handed down to us the nature of sin through his 'Adamic' curse, so did Noah, Abraham, Isaac, Jacob, Joseph, Moses, David, Solomon on down through history to Jesus and all his disciples. They all really lived. Eve too was real and I intend to look for her and meet her. I just might bite her for being so foolish as to bite into the fruit of the knowledge of good and evil. I want to give Naomi and Ruth a great big hug, and when I see Mary, I will hug her too. With tears of joy streaming down my face, I will thank her for giving birth to our Lord Jesus Christ. See what I mean, these are real people. God directed their lives to show us what He has planned for us and what is to come.

12

The Plan

Before anyone gets the idea that I am trying to re-write the Bible, I just want to get one thing clear, I am not. I just wanted to understand what is in the Bible and I went looking for the truth. In the first place, I thought God wanted us to go to heaven and be with Him, as a child that is what I had been taught to believe. As children, we were told if you were good, believed in Jesus and accepted Him as your Savior, when you die, you would go to Heaven and be with God and your family, but if you didn't repent and continued to live outside of the will of God, you would be cast into a fiery pit in Hell for eternity. I recently decided to do a search for all of the references to "heaven" and "hell" in the Bible. I didn't read all of the verses but the references to heaven were hundreds. Particularly in the Old Testament, these verses weren't talking about humans going to heaven. Most of the ones in the New Testament were the same. As for hell, there were very few mentions anywhere. I had to ask myself, if God wants us in heaven, why doesn't he say so? If hell is what we are taught, if it is so profoundly agonizing, why isn't it mentioned more and stated more clearly. I don't question God, I question our religious leaders. As I have said often in my life, who is to say which religion is God's. It seems to me that God doesn't have a religion. Man has made the "religions" of the world, not God. God's religion is just that He exists, he loves us and that we need to listen to Him. When Jesus established His "church", it wasn't a denomination or a building with a name on it, it was people following Him and His teachings.

We all know what it is to give someone our word. Even as children we know what the expression

"I give you my word" means. It means, "I promise". God's word, The Bible, in the Old Testament promises a Messiah would come. In the New Testament, Jesus fulfilled that promise. God gave His Word and He kept it. I understand now why Jesus was "THE WORD". He was the Promise that God kept. If all the religions of the world would just get that part straight and tell it without adding their little qualifiers. If only they would stop putting their little groups in boxes. If they would stop trying to make their group the *ONLY* group they want us to believe God will accept, we would all be able to come together just as Jesus wanted. All God ever wanted was for us to get along and love one another. Was Rodney King's famous line "Can't we all just get along?" prophetic? It is good advice and holds true for everyone, and not just about race.

It astounded me to learn the truth of what God's original plan was. The truth was that God never said anything about dying and going to heaven, not once, ever. Wow! Adam and Eve never thought of going to heaven. The earth was their home, not heaven. This led me to ask, "Is this still his plan"? You may think me a simpleton, I know I feel like one sometimes, but I really didn't know. I hope that you understand I am *NOT* trying to re-write God's word, but I will try to put it in my own words because I am a baby Christian who needs soft foods to be able to get the nutrition of God's word. I do hope I will be forgiven for any simplistic renderings I might get into. Just know that I am doing the best I can to get this right.

As I began my quest, I did not intend to write this book. I started 2013 with prayer and fasting praying this prayer, "God please give me clarity, discernment and purpose." beginning on January 21st. I decided I would do a 40 day fast of something that would actually be a sacrifice for me to give up. I was already on an extremely limited diet that might even test the strength of Daniel. Food was not the answer. I needed a *real* sacrifice, one that would show God I meant business. The most costly thing I could think of was to fast Glenn Beck, so that's what I gave up. My promise was to not listen to or watch Glenn for 40 days. I wanted God to know that I was serious. I needed answers and this was the only way I knew to ask for God's direction in my life. While praying and fasting, God put it in my heart and mind to write this book. Believe me, I argued with God as to why *ME*. I asked him, "Can't you find a better messenger than me? I'm not a writer. I am not a theologian or Biblical scholar". I am just a simple woman looking for the truth and doing what God is telling me to do. I have prayed long and hard to know God's will and He keeps telling me I need to do this. Honestly, I will be more than happy to get this done finally so that I can get back to being a wife and mother and whatever else God wants from me.

We are all familiar with the "In the beginning" phrase and that God gave the commands that led to the creation of all things, heaven and earth, darkness and light, land and seas, fish, birds, etc. etc. etc. Then He decided to make man and He put him in the Garden of Eden. Ok, so far so good. God said that all of these things should produce, reproduce, and fill the earth. He also said that man should cultivate this garden. Then He saw that man was alone and that he needed company and God formed from the ground every beast of the field and bird of the sky and gave them to the man so he could give them all names.

Well, God didn't think that was good enough so He made a woman for Adam. Here they were, a man and a woman in a garden and all they needed to do was to *NOT* eat from this one little tree. That's all. Anything else they could do, but *DON'T* eat from that tree!!! That shouldn't have been so hard to do.

Now, according to the Bible, Moses is told to write the name of only two trees in *Paradise*. One is the tree of the knowledge of good and evil, that's the one God says not to eat from. That's the one everyone calls an apple tree. Ha!! Whatever…….. but there is another tree. Now this tree is fine to eat from. This tree is called the *tree of life*. After Adam and Eve eat from the tree of knowledge, God bars them from eating from the tree of life, runs them out of the garden and at the east of the garden He stationed the cherubim and the flaming sword which turned every direction to guard the way to the tree of life.

But, what if they had not eaten of the tree of knowledge? What if Adam and Eve had not decided they wanted to be "like" God? What was the plan God had if they hadn't screwed up? Where would we all be right now thousands of years later? Would we be here? Would we be in heaven with God? If I look at the evidence logically, according to all of the information God gave Moses to put in the Bible, I can only conclude that God intended for humans to live on earth forever. If that is true, what about dying and going to heaven? Not that I can see. There isn't one reference to heaven being a home for man. If I follow the logic, I believe God intended for humans to fill the earth and make it a paradise over the whole planet. They wouldn't get sick, wouldn't grow old and wouldn't die. If God had wanted us in heaven, wouldn't He have put us there in the first place? If God had wanted us to die, would He have made the tree of life? In Genesis, 3:22 He even says man ***"might stretch out his hand, and take also from the tree of life and eat and live forever."***(NASB) So, man was supposed to live forever on the earth. What follows is what I believe is the truth about what God wanted eternity to look like. Also, I see a possible hint that heaven and earth are connected in the experience of Jacob beginning in Genesis 28:12 where Jacob sees a ladder leading from earth up to heaven. Then there is this passage in the book of

Luke, Chapter 23. Look at what Jesus says, when the criminal on one of the crosses next to him asked in verse 42 "Jesus, remember me when You come in Your kingdom". Jesus said in verse 43 *"Truly I say to you, today you shall be with Me in "Paradise".* (NASB)

We see the earth as a paradise the likes of which we can only describe as perfect. I'm talking everything, everywhere, is perfect. No death, no aging, no colds, flu or cancer, everyone is in perfect health. People get along with each other without fighting over this country or that, no one cares about boundaries or territories, there aren't any drug lords or terrorists, money isn't an issue, parents and children don't jockey for who is in control, food is abundant, there aren't any plant diseases to destroy a crop. Weather is perfect for every season. Animals are healthy, normal, and good to eat. The air is clean, the water is clean and all of the earth is healthy and productive.

Humans are living in perfect harmony with one another. We choose our work according to our talents. In my case, I currently am an embroiderer. I use a computer, embroidery software and computerized embroidery machines to create and produce designs and stitch them out. Some human being somewhere designed and created these various pieces of equipment and programs in order for someone like me to use them. I then can use them for my customers to make designs that decorate the things they want me to decorate. That is creative. Humans love to be creative. We have these marvelous huge brains that can learn anything we want to learn. Have you ever wondered how evolution explains the human brain? Evolution is just that, evolution. The third part of the definition is: *the gradual development of something into a more complex or better form.* So, if our brains evolved, why are they so complex and vast that we can only hope to use a fraction of it in our lifetime as it is now? I say it is because we were never meant to die. Our brains were created to be able to store an eternity of information. The world I see is filled with creative humans making whatever we want, building on each other's work, on and on. We are only limited by our creativity, and that is limitless……

Once we have reached the capacity of the earth, God will choose another planet of the many He has already created. He makes it habitable, and we humans will have readied a ship to take those who wish to go on to the next planet in line or God may just decide to put some of us on the next planet. He is God after all and can do whatever He likes. This can go on and on forever. We will planet hop for visits with relatives and friends, stay as long as we like, work at what we love to do or even learn something new to do with our time. God sets no limits to our growth. He loves to see his creation living, loving one another and learning new and wonderful things to do with our time. Oh, and an added bonus is we commune with God whenever we like and he with us just as Genesis, 3:8 describes God speaking with Adam. We will be able to speak with God and delight in His Company.

Go ahead, say it. You know you are thinking it....... You think I'm crazy, right? Yeah, you do. Well, if I'm crazy, if you do believe in God, what was the plan, if not this? When I was a child, the most common image of heaven was of angels in clouds playing harps. I could never see myself hanging out on a cloud playing a harp for eternity. Ok, so if I'm right and this was the plan, we screwed it up. Man messed up the plan God had for His creation. So, now what? What does an all-powerful God do with His creation when they mess up? Does He destroy it and start over? He could have.......but He didn't. We are still here, still messing up. Does He turn his back and walk away.......some say He has, but I don't think the All Mighty did. Does He go off in a corner of the heavens and die.........others say, yes, God is dead. Some may think that God is going to leave all as it is now, go on and on and watch us as we totally destroy ourselves and this planet. No, I say God had a plan and I don't think He will allow us to stop that plan. He didn't make us, the earth, the sun and moon, all the stars and planets and *EVERYTHING* just to let us screw it up and give up. This is not what an all-powerful God would do.

So, according to the Bible, He decided to save his creation.......mankind. How? In Genesis He began to implement the plan to restore the plan.......with a sacrifice. Wait, what? A sacrifice, a symbolic act. Not of appeasement like pagans do, but a sacrifice for consecration and atonement. A pagan god would demand a sacrifice of an animal, a child or a virgin to keep his followers in line. *"Kill me something or I will destroy you,"* was the thought, but not our God. The *ONE TRUE GOD* Jehovah, the God of the Bible, began the practice of a sacrifice in the Garden of Eden. Yes.....look it up. Adam and Eve have just disobeyed God's command not to eat of the tree of knowledge. They go......."*Um......we are naked.....um.... that's nasty. We had better put something on before God sees us."* After telling God all that they have just done, oh and by the way, instead of admitting they were wrong, Adam blames God saying **"The woman whom You gave to be with me, she gave me from the tree, and I ate"** (NASB).... which basically was Adam saying "Well, you gave me the woman and she made me do it, so it's *your* fault." Eve, at least, has the decency to blame the snake, but neither one say they screwed up or that they were sorry. Nope... but if they had, maybe we wouldn't all be imperfect today. However, that's another story altogether.

Getting back to the first sacrifice, God sees that

Adam and Eve have covered themselves with fig leaves and before He forces them to leave, He tells them what their fate will be. Adam will work very hard for the rest of his life just to eat and Eve will have great pain having children. He then tells the snake that he will crawl on the ground and be beneath all others, adding in Genesis 3:15, he gives us a prophesy about the future. God tells the snake that He has *"put enmity between your seed and her seed; He shall crush you on the head, and you shall bruise him on the heal."* (NKJV) This is God telling us the prophesy of the coming battle between Jesus and Satan. In Genesis 3:21 it says *"The Lord God made garments of skin for Adam and his wife, and clothed them."* (NIV) So, God killed animals for their skins to cover the sin Adam and Eve committed. He used these skins as atonement for their sin and as a consecration of their lives from that point on. I can imagine a spotless lamb chosen by God to redeem the sin of Adam and Eve just as He would sacrifice His Son, *The Lamb of God,* for our sins later with the life of Jesus. At that moment, God demonstrates what He will do to save His creation from themselves.

I contend that God has been working His plan from the moment Adam and Eve would not ask God to forgive them for breaking His commandment not to eat of the tree of knowledge. If only they had said they were sorry, God could have forgiven them and all would have gone on as God intended. I can see the Plan just as clearly as the words on this page. God wants His children, His people to live according to His plan here on His earth. In peace with one another, His will is for all of us to be restored to perfect health to live on the restored earth, multiplying and filling the earth with loving humans. It is simple, but it isn't so easy to do. This Plan will take time to complete.

In my simple mind, putting all of this into perspective in my own life, the scenario would go something like this: My unbelieving husband, that beautiful 21 year old that made my heart leap 46 years ago, would be restored. I see him reading my words and realizing God is real, and He loves us all and wants us to live, not die. In the life to come, he would be with me, our daughters and whoever else makes it into the restored life, next life or whatever it is called. My three daughters would be restored to perfect health. In this life, they all have or had endometriosis. They have suffered the pain and agony of this hateful disease that made them unable to have children. My poor Bonnie died of a drug overdose. In my mind, since I have no idea what was in her heart when she passed and how God viewed her, she comes back and is a healthy, happy, a perfect woman able to have as many children as she wants. Her hysterectomy would be reversed, her addiction to pain pills gone along with her anger at others for what she suffered in her tortured mind. Free from pain, my beautiful, solid, responsible oldest daughter Rhonda would be restored to perfect health without the endometriosis that took one ovary and rendered her unlikely to have children. Finally, my beautiful baby Sandra who seemed to suffer most from the pain and agony of this insidious disease would be fully restored. She will have her ovaries restored along with all of the rest of the reproductive system taken from her bit by bit until there was nothing left. This hideous endometriosis has affected her bowel and bladder with IBS and IC as well, but this too will disappear. With perfect health, she will be able to have all the children she and her husband Robbie want. Since we all will be restored to perfect health and youth, I see no reason for me and my husband not to have more beautiful children including having the son we would have liked to have had in this life. You see, to me, all of this is possible when God restores His plan for mankind.

Many believe we are living in the last days. I certainly can't say that for sure even though I feel it is a possibility. I don't know when these things will happen but, since the end of WWII, we humans have been steadily moving toward our own demise. Our world is more dangerous than ever before with hot spots on nearly every continent. This is not even arguable. The fact that we know how to kill each other on a worldwide scale so quickly, easily and efficiently 10 times over makes it more likely to happen in the near future. Some would say, "we'll never go that far". Really? All we need for this to begin is one little madman who doesn't give a rat's rear end what happens to anyone else as long as he gets what he wants. Does anyone know of a world leader who fits that description? Can you think of anyone who would do this in order for his prophet to return? Actually, I can think of a number of little dictators who would love nothing better than to have the power of life and death over the entire earth. Heady stuff, power. Man was never meant to have that kind of power.

God has His own plans and humankind cannot change those plans. Try as he might, man can build his monuments, tear them down and build them up again, but he cannot bring peace to the world. No United Nations, no World Health Organization, no International Peace Organization, no International Monetary Fund, World Trade Organization or any other manmade bureaucracy has ever brought about peace. Only God can do that. God doesn't need us to do anything. Face it. He will restore His creation without our help. We can either go along with Him or suffer the consequences. However, when? How long will God wait?

If we want to know when, I believe it will be soon. I believe I will live to see it because of the increase in speed of man's ability to destroy themselves and the signs Jesus gave for the last days. Look in the book of Mark, Chapter 13 and read Jesus' words regarding the last days. Also, in the sermon series entitled ***The Coming Four Blood Moons***, Pastor John Hagee gives a clear and convincing delivery of facts from the Bible backed by secular sources regarding signs of the last days and the coming events that will affect mankind. I recommend you find Pastor's book ***The Coming Four Blood Moons*** and read it. We all know that what is happening on earth now cannot go on without consequences. The United States cannot continue to print money based on nothing without causing hyperinflation. Hyperinflation means that the money we have in our pockets or bank accounts will be worthless. The *tsunami* is coming...... nothing can stop it. The worst part is no one is even trying to. Other nations around the world are doing the same. Nation after nation is spending money at an alarming rate, rogue nations are arming themselves with weapons that will kill the maximum number of people, old hatreds are resurfacing and peoples all around the world feel the growing threats like never before in human history. The same is true with the coming of Jesus Christ. He is coming...... you cannot stop it, you can either believe it or not, that is up to you. I have already told you my feelings about our founding being a part of God's plan. I now propose that the end is near for a new reason. Jesus commanded his disciples to tell the good news of His life and death to the nations of the earth. The United States has made that more possible. The message of Jesus has spread more readily around the world for all to hear since the founding of our nation. Since the days of the disciples, the return of Christ was a question that believers have asked and wondered about throughout the ages. When asked, Jesus himself did not know but said only the Father knows the day. I now think that all the peoples of the earth have had the chance to hear the Word of God and decide if they believe it or not. If I am right, this may be what God has waited for. He has stayed His hand just as He did for Sodom and Gomorra. Once He saw there was no one else to save, He destroyed them for their wickedness. Once all the peoples of the earth have had the chance to decide to accept God's word or not, He will give the command for Christ to return. In any case, time is running out whether we like it or not.

This is what I personally believe: those who have put their faith in Jesus and not in men, have accepted Him as their redeemer, will be those spoken of in 1 Thessalonians 4:17. ***"Then we who are alive and remain will be caught up together with them in the clouds to meet the Lord in the air, and so we shall always be with the Lord."*** This is widely called *The Rapture*. Please understand me, I see this as a rescue mission because, according to the Bible, what follows will be dreadful. To those left on earth, they may certainly feel as if all hell is breaking loose. The Bible describes this as a *great tribulation* and it will last for 7 years. Then Jesus returns to start the final phase of the restoration of the earth and begin His thousand-year reign.

Are we living in the last days? Again, I don't know, but Jesus spoke of the last days as coming when we least expect it. He spoke of the flood of Noah and how people were doing their everyday things up until the end when they were washed away. He spoke of the time as coming like a thief in the night. He said in Mathew 24:44 *"So you also must be ready, because the Son of Man will come at an hour when you do not expect him."* He listed all the things that must happen: Matthew 24:1 **Jesus left the temple and was walking away when his disciples came up to him to call his attention to its buildings. 2** *"Do you see all these things?"* **he asked.** *"Truly I tell you, not one stone here will be left on another; everyone will be thrown down."*

3 As Jesus was sitting on the Mount of Olives, the disciples came to him privately. *"Tell us,"* **they said,** *"when will this happen, and what will be the sign of your coming and of the end of the age?"*

4 Jesus answered: *"Watch out that no one deceives you. 5 For many will come in my name, claiming, 'I am the Messiah,' and will deceive many. 6 You will hear of wars and rumors of wars, but see to it that you are not alarmed. Such things must happen, but the end is still to come. 7 Nation will rise against nation, and kingdom against kingdom. There will be famines and earthquakes in various places. 8 All these are the beginning of birth pains.*

9 "Then you will be handed over to be persecuted and put to death, and you will be hated by all nations because of me. 10 At that time many will turn away from the faith and will betray and hate each other, 11 and many false prophets will appear and deceive many people. 12 Because of the increase of wickedness, the love of most will grow cold, 13 but the one who stands firm to the end will be saved. 14 And this gospel of the kingdom will be preached in the whole world as a testimony to all nations, and then the end will come.

15 "So when you see standing in the holy place 'the abomination that causes desolation,'[a] spoken of through the prophet Daniel— **let the reader understand***— 16 then let those who are in Judea flee to the mountains. 17 Let no one on the housetop go down to take anything out of the house. 18 Let no one in the field go back to get their cloak. 19 How dreadful it will be in those days for pregnant women and nursing mothers! 20 Pray that your flight will not take place in winter or on the Sabbath. 21 For then there will be great distress, unequaled from the beginning of the world until now—and never to be equaled again.*

22 "If those days had not been cut short, no one

would survive, but for the sake of the elect those days will be shortened. 23 At that time if anyone says to you, 'Look, here is the Messiah!' or, 'There he is!' do not believe it. 24 For false messiahs and false prophets will appear and perform great signs and wonders to deceive, if possible, even the elect. 25 See, I have told you ahead of time.

26 "So if anyone tells you, 'There he is, out in the wilderness,' do not go out; or, 'Here he is, in the inner rooms,' do not believe it. 27 For as lightning that comes from the east is visible even in the west, so will be the coming of the Son of Man. 28 Wherever there is a carcass, there the vultures will gather.

29 "Immediately after the distress of those days the sun will be darkened, and the moon will not give its light; the stars will fall from the sky, and the heavenly bodies will be shaken.'[b]30 "Then will appear the sign of the Son of Man in heaven. And then all the peoples of the earth[c] will mourn when they see the Son of Man coming on the clouds of heaven, with power and great glory.[d] 31 And he will send his angels with a loud trumpet call, and they will gather his elect from the four winds, from one end of the heavens to the other.

32 "Now learn this lesson from the fig tree: As soon as its twigs get tender and its leaves come out, you know that summer is near. 33 Even so, when you see all these things, you know that it[e] is near, right at the door. 34 Truly I tell you, this generation will certainly not pass away until all these things have happened. 35 Heaven and earth will pass away, but my words will never pass away."

What do I believe? What is my religion? I believe in the God of the bible, Jehovah God, the God of Abraham, Isaac and Jacob. The Jews are the chosen people of God and Jehovah promised the land of Israel to them in an eternal covenant. It says so in God's word. I believe Jesus is my redeemer who came to save us all from sin and death. I have no "religion" as I believe denominations are not from God, but are ideas man has made to make himself special. Religions established by men serve to divide us by telling their members their way is the only way to God. I realize this will tick some people off, but to those people I would say show me where in the Bible God says He is a Catholic, Baptist, Methodist or Pentecostal. Name any of the religions of the world and I will say show me which one is the only one using God's word to do so. You cannot because it isn't there. Jesus was a Jew and came to redeem the Jews as well as the gentiles. Do I have a scripture for that? Yes, there are many. Paul wrote about this in his letter to the congregation in Rome. You should read all of the book of *Romans* but, in Romans Chapter 11 verses 11-15 it says regarding the Jews: ***"I say then, have they stumbled that they should fall? Certainly not! But through their fall, to provoke them to jealousy, salvation has come to the Gentiles. 12 Now if their fall is riches for the world, and their failure riches for the Gentiles, how much more their fullness!***

"13 For I speak to you Gentiles; inasmuch as I am an apostle to the Gentiles, I magnify my ministry, 14 if by any means I may provoke to jealousy those who are my flesh and save some of them. 15 For if their being cast away is the reconciling of the world, what will their acceptance be but life from the

dead?" (NKJV)

In an article from Wikipedia on Franklin it says: When he stopped attending church, Benjamin Franklin wrote in his autobiography *... **Sunday being my studying day, I never was without some religious principles. I never doubted, for instance, the existence of the Deity; that He made the world, and governed it by His providence; that the most acceptable service of God was the doing good to man; that our souls are immortal; and that all crime will be punished, and virtue rewarded, either here or hereafter.*** What does he mean? He is saying there is a God and He created everything. God decides everything and He wants us to be good to each other. Our souls do not die and we will be punished for our sins and we will be rewarded for the good we do. All of this is biblical no matter the 'religion'. So, I say, follow the bible not men.

I am now 63 years old and finally ready to confess to God that I haven't always been the best version of myself. My life has been a mass of confusion and contradictions that led to needless suffering on my part and on the part of my children and my husband. My poor children deserved a better mother. My husband deserved a better wife. My mother and father deserved a better daughter. I confess that I should have done better and make no excuses, but ask all of those in my life that I have wronged who are still alive to forgive me, and I pray that God forgives me for my sins. I pray that the rest of my life will be what God wants it to be and I will serve God, my family and my fellow man to the best of my ability always and unto the end of this life. I know that I am not worthy on my own but only through the gift of life through the redemptive blood of Jesus Christ who is my Savior. As yet, I have not found a church to join although I am an honorary member of the Cornerstone Church in San Antonio, Texas. I have no plans to join a religion since religions seem to have stumbled me in the past. I don't want to go there again. However, when I am in Central, I do receive a great deal of spiritual blessings visiting Journey Church. The congregation there has welcomed me with opened arms and Pastor Jay Coleman has helped me by being an ear when I needed someone to talk to.

When I began writing this over a year ago, I was convinced time was running out. My main concern was whether I would be able to fulfill my wish to be baptized before it was too late. Fortunately, I was wrong. We are all still awaiting God's time to bring forth His will. Therefore, I was able to fulfill my plans to go down into the Amite River to be baptized and born again with faith believing through Jesus Christ on May 19, 2013 for the third and final time. This time it is *REAL* and I know it to be true.

I pray to Jehovah God that I will be able to live in such a way as to be a better wife, mother and friend to all in the name of Jesus Christ, AMEN.

THE END

Conclusion

I would like to thank those without whom I would never have been able to begin this work, let alone finish it. First, let me thank God for waking me up and asking me to write it in the first place. Next, I would like to thank my husband Gary and my daughters Rhonda and Sandra who have been my support all these years with love and understanding. I would especially like to thank Glenn Beck and his Mercury Radio Arts organization and The Blaze TV for listening to the Holy Spirit and bringing truth to a world that is upside down. Through the years Glenn and crew brought the likes of Jonathan Cahn of Hope of the World and author of *The Harbinger*; David Barton, historian, founder of WallBuilders, author of *The Jefferson Lies* and numerous other books; John and Matthew Hagee of Cornerstone Church in San Antonio, Texas and their internet broadcasts on *GETV* as well as many excellent spiritual books into my life. I would like to include Dr. Mike Evans, author of *Living in the F.O.G. (Favor of God)*, one of many inspirational books and founder of the Jerusalem Prayer Team as well as other bible scholars Glenn introduced me to that have helped me find the truth about God that would change my life. I pray that I might someday personally thank them all.

I would also like to thank my sister Shirley who was the first to read this and made me feel as if I had not wasted my time. I frequently doubt myself and she helped me feel confidence at a time when I needed it. I can say the same about Jodi from Journey Church in Central, LA who didn't know it at the time but his encouragement made me want to go back and finish what I started. I will add, as well, Pastors Jay and Stacey Coleman of Journey Church for their spiritual guidance when I needed it then and now.

There were many more tiny moments when I could hear the voice of God speaking through others encouraging me to press on when I would lose my way. My neighbors Linda Lyons and Lynn Plaisance, two of my biggest cheerleaders, have given me more encouragement than I can possibly relay here and I cannot thank them enough. Finally, I will thank my daughter Rhonda for proofing this tomb as well as listening to my agonies as I worked through the pangs of giving birth to this book.

I wish I could list all of those who have given me encouragement and thank them too, but I cannot as I am not a true journal keeper. I wish that I were so this could have been a better book. With that said, I would like to finish by saying I love you, dear reader, and pray God blesses you as well.

ABOUT THE AUTHOR

Linda Habisreitinger is a wife and mother making her mark as a home based embroiderer with her business ***Embroidery Designs and Monogramming by Linda*** in her suburban neighborhood outside of New Orleans, Louisiana where she lives with her husband Gary. You are invited to visit her website at www.embroidery-linda.com.

Her first attempt at writing came while she attended West Jefferson Technical Institute with a class in creative writing as part of her secretarial course. Later, she penned a tongue-in- cheek article entitled "How I Lost My Mind to Machine Embroidery" for an embroidery website. *Wake Up Dummy…It's Me, GOD!* is her first book but it may not be her last.

She is mostly self-educated, having dropped out of high school when she and her husband were married. She earned her *GED* a year later. Having widely traveled during the years her husband was in the military, she came into contact with a diverse cross section of society. Since opening her embroidery business, she has enjoyed meeting and working with the best customers anyone could hope to have.

In later years, she and her husband and daughter Rhonda have widely traveled the U.S. and cruised in the Caribbean and the Mediterranean. Her last cruise was on the Costa Concordia, November 2009 before it struck land and sank in January of 2012 off the cost of Isola del Giglio, Tuscany, Italy. Her two surviving daughters currently live in the Baton Rouge area.

~~~~~~

Made in the USA
Lexington, KY
04 October 2014